Praise for *Findir*

"Dr. Bruce Jackson is an international expert in leadership training and optimal performance. His new book offers effective and essential skills for improving human performance. I recommend it to all parents, teachers, coaches, students, and athletes. Get this book and go Find Your Flow!"

  – Christopher Barden, Ph.D., J.D.

"Summiting Mt. Everest with 19 people, especially with the first blind man to accomplish the feat, is about knowing your assets and liabilities--both inside and out. In the summit of life you need to do the same analysis. Read and apply the tools in this book and begin planning for your own personal summit."

  – Jeff Evans, Everest Expedition Leader, corporate speaker, physician assistant

"*Finding Your Flow* is a book dedicated to helping anyone identify the common factors of high performance. It is a must for readers interested in beginning their self-development journey."

  – Alan Fine, CEO/President, InsideOut Development

"No fluff. No psychobabble. Just a solid, transformational guide for life and leadership."

  – Dr. Kerry Joels, International Organizational Consultant

"*Finding Your Flow* distills the qualities of personal leadership to their pure essence, teaching you an easy way to implement positive change in all aspects of life: business, personal, and spiritual."

  – Ernest M. John, Director of Research and Development/Engineering, Action Target Inc.

"By applying the tools and methods of *Finding Your Flow*, the budding high performer will possess the knowledge and skills necessary to master peak performance within any life arena."

– Dr. Jim Loehr, Renowned performance psychologist and best-selling author

"A fully connected focus is an essential skill for performance excellence, quality learning and positive living. *Finding Your Flow* takes us another positive step forward in this direction."

– Dr. Terry Orlick, Author of *In Pursuit of Excellence, Positive Living Skills and Embracing your Potential*

"Focus and being in the zone is what the Olympics are all about. If you want to be an Olympian in anything, *Finding Your Flow* will help you discover that 'one thing.'"

– Noelle Pikus-Pace, U.S. Olympian (Skeleton)

"Going far beyond theory, *Finding Your Flow* breaks down the process of high performance into steps any dedicated reader can accomplish."

– Susan K. Perry, Ph.D., author of *Writing in Flow* and Creativity Blogger at PsychologyToday.com.

"*Finding Your Flow* provides a road map for peak performance through a straight forward approach that will benefit not only the newcomer to self-development, but also the seasoned expert who is looking for the edge to take their performance to the next level."

– Rod B. Streets, MPA, SSBB, CMA, CFM - Manufacturing Finance Executive

"While working with Olympic athletes and performing artists from many countries, I found that getting more control over the flow state is a need among almost everyone. This book will help peak performers as well as the general public to establish a life in which flow can become a part of everyday living."

– Lars-Eric Unestähl, Ph.D, Swedish Olympic Team Psychologist

"The *Finding Your Flow* model is straightforward and easy for our managers to understand and apply in both personal and business situations."

– Jeff Weber, VP People, Ancestry.com

"Many people jump into personal development training without the self-awareness to choose the right method of practice. *Finding Your Flow* provides just this awareness."

– Dr. Steve Wilkinson, Director of Tennis & Life Camps

"It's a huge treat to have an extremely important, yet complex, subject such as *flow* made accessible via an insightful analysis. Better yet, this book provides a practical roadmap that enables anyone who is serious to expand their flow."

– Dr. Jack Zenger, CEO, Zenger-Folkman, co-author of the best-selling *The Extraordinary Leader* and *The Inspiring Leader*.

"Few people have gone as far and as deep studying what liberates people from mediocrity as Bruce Jackson has. Pay attention!"

– Nathaniel Zinsser, PhD, CC-AASP, Director, Performance Enhancement Program, United States Military Academy (West Point)

Finding Your Flow:

How to Identify Your Flow Assets and Liabilities—
the Keys to Peak Performance Every Day

by

Bruce H. Jackson, Ph.D.

FOREWORD BY STEPHEN R. COVEY

The Institute of
Applied Human Excellence

The Institute of Applied Human Excellence

www.theiahe.com

6193 West Ridge. Rd.

Highland, UT 84003

brucehjackson@gmail.com

801-358-8450

Library of Congress Control Number on file with Publisher

"Finding Your Flow," by Bruce H. Jackson. ISBN 978-1-60264-775-6 (softcover); 978-1-60264-784-8 (casebound).

Manufactured in the United States of America.

TABLE OF CONTENTS

FOREWORD

Quite simply, the main quest of humanity is to discover its potential. In every arena and stage of life the human spirit seeks to identify the unique contributions that it was designed to make. In my study and teaching of effective human behavior and relations I have discovered that the elements of success are common to all men and women, girls and boys. There are principles and practices that, if understood, can be applied by anyone to maximize their effectiveness on the job, on the playing field, and in life.

You may have discovered that throughout your life you have experienced moments—even hours, days and weeks—where tremendous focus, meaning, enjoyment, purpose graced the life-stage you were performing on. You may have discovered that these were special moments where everything just came together and gave you a glimpse of what you were made of and what you were designed to accomplish. You may have recognized these moments as "peak experiences" or moments of "flow".

When you boil it all down, human growth and effectiveness come from our best and most profound moments—even our moments of flow. When I wrote the *7 Habits of Highly Effective People*, my objective was to illuminate and simplify the key principles of individual, interpersonal and collective effectiveness. The very elements that comprise this effectiveness are many and vast, yet they are unique and personal to each person. As you read, study, and apply the methods within the powerful book you're holding, you will come to understand yourself and your environment more deeply.

Finding Your Flow is a book with a grand goal and purpose: to help raise your level of awareness regarding the building blocks of effectiveness, then to help you sort out these building blocks in order to identify *your* most important personal development plan of action. You might, therefore, think of this book as a pre-cursor or primer to your personal leadership training.

The motivated reader who seeks to improve his/her performance in any life arena can use this book as a starting point and framework for a life-long pursuit of self-understanding, excellence, happiness, and for living life in crescendo!

- Dr. Stephen R. Covey

Section I – Introducing Flow

CHAPTER 1: From Low to High

I once asked my father to describe a time in his life when he was at his very best. Without hesitation, he said that his four years serving as a PT boat commander in Europe and Africa were when he had his most profound and engaging personal experiences. This was a surprise, so I dug deeper and asked, "What made the war so profound for you?" It soon became clear why those years were so transforming for him.

For most people, war is a time of great personal sacrifice, uncertainty, stress, and fear. For my father, war was all of those things, but it was also something more: He felt great purpose, his days were bound by clear roles and measurable goals. He was driven by powerful motives, and he got precise feedback for his actions. Pursuing the enemy, managing other men, being ready for action at any time—these requirements took full powers of mind and body. They pushed the limits of his mental, emotional, and physical capacity, all for the greater good of his country—something bigger than himself. In essence for much of those years, my father was "in the zone." He was, in fact, in *flow*.

The Bad Day

Because I think you'll find it enlightening and perhaps a stark contrast to the story above, I'd like to share how my personal interest in flow began.

It wasn't until I was about 16 that I really noticed it. I was scheduled to play in the Stillwater Open, a tennis tournament consisting of eight schools. As the number one player from my school, I was paired against the number one players from eight of the leading high schools in my region. Our number two player played all of the number twos and so on down the ladder.

The day before, our team had played a small school located outside the local farming community. None of us had expected much competition that day. Dressed confidently, I met my opponent—a short stocky kid who didn't look much like a tennis player—an old racket, tan socks, that sort of thing.

It didn't take long before I began to get frustrated. I wasn't playing particularly well, and this kid wasn't missing much. His game wasn't pretty, but he ran down every ball and got it back over the net. Soon I found myself on the losing side of the match, and my emotions got the best of me. No longer was I focused on the ball, a game plan, my breathing, or anything else under my control. Rather, I was consumed with frustration and anger. In a flash the game was over, and I was left bewildered and my ego shattered. I was sure my tennis rackets were going to find their way into the nearest trash can.

After a cooling-off period, Coach came up to me and asked, "What happened?" "I don't know," I said. "I just stunk it up out there today. I didn't estimate my opponent's persistence. I got frustrated, I didn't move. I wasn't focused."

"Well, be ready for tomorrow's tournament in Stillwater. We're leaving early." Playing the next day's tournament was the last thing I wanted to do, but there was no getting around it.

From Food Fight to Flow

We were up early and met at the courts. I drove one car, and Carter, our number two man, another, and Coach a third. With each of us carrying a third of the team, we were off to Stillwater, about an hour and a half away.

About 30 miles into the trip, it happened. Carter positioned his red Buick in front of my mother's pea green wagon. I saw some commotion in their car, followed by a rolling down of the window. "What the—!" At 65 miles an hour, a large red and white projectile found its way onto the windshield of my car. I couldn't make it out. "It's a strawberry!" someone said. "With whipped cream!" said another. "They're throwing their lunch at us." It was war! Soon another strawberry came flying, then another, two direct hits and we couldn't do anything about it. We were boxed in. The windshield wipers were working double-time and I was about out of fluid. What a mess.

"Pull out your lunches, boys," I yelled. "It's payback time!" When I saw an opening in traffic, I took it. We flanked our teammates on the left, then took the lead position, all windows lowered. Bologna slices were flung, along with everything else we had in the car. We made multiple direct hits, and we could see the look on their faces. Sixty more miles to go and the party was just getting started. It was the funniest moment of our young lives! We laughed until we cried. Never had a food fight escalated to such a magnitude on the I35W highway.

We food-fighters were the last two cars to pull into the tennis complex, and we were late. All the athletes were lined up and taking directions from the tournament director. The only two parking spaces lay right in front of the entire group. Coach was already there, and he was beside himself with anger. Everyone stared at us, not because we were late, but because our cars were completely covered in food.

The chastisement was swift and harsh, but we had a tournament to play. We were all assigned to our courts and paired with our opponents. It was about 70 degrees, the sun was finding its way to the sky, and the day was beautiful. With laughter in our hearts, the mood was set.

As the matches progressed, one 8-game pro-set after another, I noticed something: I couldn't miss a ball. My focus was spot on. I was not only having fun out there, but I was moving exceptionally well. Nothing was distracting me—nothing from

5

the inside and nothing from the outside. All I dealt with was the ball and where it was going to be placed. Each shot was practically perfect, and before I knew it, I had won the tournament. Eight matches to zero, with less than 20 points lost in the entire day!

The previous day, I had struggled against an unknown and relatively inexperienced player, yet today I walked off the court with the most profound sense of personal excellence and control I had ever felt. I sat down and tried to dissect the experience and tease out what I had done differently.

Was it my mood? Certainly I felt happy and calm. It was all part of the security you feel when connecting deeply with friends and those you most care about. This feeling of calm seemed to modify my mood and my thoughts. No longer was I there to justify my existence. Instead I could enjoy the moment, play the game, and simply have fun. I didn't have to prove my value to the world through my tennis playing. Letting go of the outcome and everything outside myself allowed me to focus on the only things that mattered: the ball, the court, and playing each point as if nothing else existed. With such an attitude and focus there was little that might get in my way—no unrealistic expectations, just *bounce* and *hit*. At that point, winning and losing simply took care of themselves.

Of course there was a bit more to it. For example, I later understood how much it helped that my goals and objectives were clear (to triumph over my opponent, be ranked in the top 10), there were boundaries to the game (lines and space surrounded by a fence), clear rules (scoring, time between points, etiquette), strategies for engagement (exposing the weaknesses of my opponent), feedback (statistics, shot percentages, final score), and so on. I truly enjoyed hitting the ball and moving my body to execute each shot with precision, and I always knew where I stood relative to my final objective. These same factors became even more prevalent in my college years and later as I had the chance to play world-class players. Although the intensity and rigor of these games were unmatched, the principles and practices were the same. How fascinating that the arenas of tennis and war, so different, yet so alike when it came to inducing flow.

Those new and simple insights were very powerful. I had learned something and I was determined to capture it, bottle it up, and use it the next time I stepped onto the court.

In my life-long pursuit of such special moments, it has become clear to me that almost any activity, or meaningful life arena (MLA) as I like to call them, can become a place for the expression of personal excellence—or what many call flow, peak experience, or being in the zone. These are enjoyable states, often setting the stage for higher levels of performance or satisfaction and the utilization of one's greatest gifts or talents. This is what the esteemed psychologist Abraham Maslow called self-actualization.

Once you've experienced flow you will find it highly attractive—everything seems to fall into place. These moments and hours are so desirable that many people seek to engineer their lives around them.

There is a problem, however, one that we are going to explore and aim to resolve within this book. It's that flow can be an elusive state of mind, one that makes an entrance and an exit, usually without invitation or announcement. It is the Holy Grail of experiences, one that every athlete, astronaut, surgeon, military pilot, Formula One driver, firefighter, poet, and dancer wishes they could tap into at a moment's notice. These can be difficult moments to catch and hold on to, but I believe that's only because most of us lack the necessary insight.

The fact is, finding your flow is possible—even probable—when you become aware of and commit to certain deliberate practices.

How to Use This Book

Kurt Lewin, the well-known organizational theorist and practitioner, said, "Nothing is as practical as a good theory." And it was Oliver Wendell Holmes who remarked, "I wouldn't give a fig for the simplicity on this side of complexity, but I would give my right arm for the simplicity on the far side of complexity." You might combine both comments and say that while good theories are useful, they must be simple enough to apply in everyday life.

Flow theory, in fact, derives from a rather simple premise—that deep focus is valuable. Look a bit deeper and we find a holistic framework that gives incredible insight into the nature of human potential.

Beyond theory and the hundreds of articles and books on the subject of flow, I looked deep into people's experiences, interviewing more than 100 men and women to identify the many principles, practices, and strategies that individuals actually use to get and stay in a flow state on a regular basis. These interviewees included students as young as 15 and people as old as 95, with distinct groups that included high school students, college students, professionals, and what I will be referring to as the more "experienced" group of individuals at least 65 years old.

From controlling tension to visualization and from getting fired up to developing personal rituals, humans have an endless capacity to discover and build personal strategies for finding flow. By better understanding the major principles and concepts of flow as they relate to your own Meaningful Life Arenas, you will have the tools you need to create your own Personal Flow Formula.

As you read this book, let it serve as a starting point for your journey to personal excellence. Consider it a kind of workshop-in-a-book, as I've modeled it after the popular workshops and classes I've been giving for six years to both college students and professionals in many fields.

Throughout the rest of **Section I**, which is especially aimed at readers less familiar with flow, I'll be sharing information about flow, including what it is exactly and what it feels like when you're in it so you can recognize it. You're in charge, so feel free to skim these basics, though I believe you'll learn something new no matter what your background is.

In **Section II**, you'll get an overview of flow strategies, including external, internal, and time-based strategies.

Then, in **Section III**, we'll seriously tackle how you can find your own flow. We'll begin with a thorough self-analysis, followed by identifying your personal Flow Assets and Flow Liabilities. Then you'll learn how to build your Personal Flow Formula.

And finally, in **Section IV**, we'll go even further in exploring and demonstrating how you can take action and become conscious of your own competence, eventually learning how to become your own best coach and benefit from flow whenever you choose. Enjoy the journey.

CHAPTER 2: Nuts and Bolts of Flow

Everyday life is filled with average experiences. We wake up, shower, brush our teeth, pick out our clothes, eat our breakfast, kiss our loved ones, leave for work, and so on through all the other habits that sustain our day.

Yet certain experiences stand out from the rest. They look different, feel different, and often give us insights into our own potential. Perhaps this was the day you were giving that big presentation. You spent months preparing for it, doing the research, building your slides, speaking with colleagues, double-checking your figures, visualizing the moment when you'd be in front of the room fielding questions with tremendous ease, impressing your colleagues. Or perhaps you were playing racquetball, running, or simply walking in the park, or involved in an interpersonal experience such as enjoying a deep conversation or engaging with your children on the playground. And everything came together just as you imagined. Time flew by. You were completely absorbed in the moment, in flow.

Background of the Concept

Whether you call it flow, being in the zone, peak engagement, or any of the other phrases that have been applied to this desirable state of mind, the phenomenon isn't new. Long before recent times, in fact as early as 521 C.E., Buddha himself recognized the importance of training both the mind and body in the pursuit of developing the whole self.[1]

Over the past forty years, many great theorists have delved into the science of how such states of consciousness operate, though not as many have translated these models into useful tools for everyday use. Since the early 1970s, most notably in Eastern Europe and Russia, most Olympic athletes trained both the mind and body together in order to reach peak engagement and flow.[2] If you look at the history of the Olympic Games at that time, you will discover most of the gold medals going to the Russians and the East Germans. This was no accident.

In modern day arenas, NASA regularly trains their astronauts, using their giant Neutral Buoyancy Laboratory pool in order to simulate movement in space. In addition, they use techniques of mental simulation, emotional control, attention and focus, and pre-performance planning in order to ensure the success of every shuttle mission. Similarly, these performance technologies are used every day by professional dancers, musicians, surgeons, police and fire departments, the military, business managers and executives, and performers in every other arena.

In preparation for each of Christi's auctions, for example, Christopher Burge enters the stage with a clear goal in mind—to exceed his $1,000,000 per minute average. Prior to each show, he carefully plans for every event to ensure that each piece of art will be auctioned off at the proper time. He enters the stage with a snifter of Scotch to ease his nerves while centering himself to focus on the task at hand. He quickly seeks to exceed the reserve price on each item in order to build momentum and to exceed his sales goals. He explains that facilitating an auction contains elements of playing to a crowd in the ancient Roman coliseum: "They want blood or thrills."

During the auction he connects with each member of the audience by using his hands, his body, and his eyebrows. He injects energy and banter to adjust the mood of the crowd and uses his skills of communication to invoke a sense of friendly competition. During transaction after transaction he works the room until everything has moved. He then exits the stage completely exhausted. After each show, he painstakingly reviews the auction on video, analyzing his performance, learning as he goes and preparing for the next event. Clearly the auction arena provides the context for Burge to find his flow.

In a very different arena, Viktor Frankl, the great humanist, spoke in much detail about the mental, emotional, even spiritual practices he and other inmates used to find meaning and endure the physical and emotional abuses of life in a Nazi concentration camp. While such terrible events can hardly be likened to the exhilaration and joys of competition, they nonetheless have the potential to instruct and engage. Be it good or bad, positive or negative, fulfilling or anxiety provoking, any Meaningful Life Arena can provide a context from which one can seek learning and understanding.

Much has been discovered about flow from motivational theorists, humanistic psychologists, existentialists, and others who have studied the nature of creativity, play, performance, self-actualization, and happiness, and who today make up the Positive Psychology movement.[3] Early investigations focused on intrinsic motivation, including the study of chess players, rock climbers, surgeons, musicians, athletes, and artists. Mihaly Csikszentmihalyi (pronounced: chick, sent, me, hi) studied the nature of intrinsic motivation, referring to the autotelic personality (*auto* = self; *telos* = goal), describing individuals who were engaged in the activities for their own sake instead of for some external purpose.[4] After conducting and analyzing interviews with hundreds of individuals within several life arenas, he named the concept "flow" because individuals used that word to describe the kinds of experiences they were having.[5]

The Benefits of Flow

Why is flow so sought after? Because it's an altered state of consciousness wherein performance level, satisfaction, and happiness all rise. You become one with whatever you're doing, you feel utterly absorbed and enjoy intrinsic rewards as you do the activity. Your skills sharpen to meet the demands of the challenges, and everything falls into place. In essence, it is like tapping into your best self, where who you are and what you are doing fall into perfect alignment and harmony.

The times we find flow are the great moments, the great days, the great experiences that we remember. These are the experiences that stand out above the rest and give us a small glimpse into our potential.

Studies have found that as many as 85 per cent of individuals have experienced flow at least once in their life.[6] Some report reaching it on a daily basis.[7] From children and teenagers to the elderly, athletes to farmers, and a growing number of ethnic populations, flow seems to provide a universal experience that anyone can tap into.

In summarizing the universal nature of flow, Csikszentmihalyi states it most beautifully:

> It is the same experience that the artist has as he works on the canvas, or the athlete during a race. It is how mountain climbers explain why they climb, how scientists describe the process of research, or surgeons whose challenging operations feel "like taking narcotics." All of these activities provide a common expanded state of consciousness that is so enjoyable that often no other reward than continuing the experience is required to keep it going.[8]

Whether your goals are to increase your focus on the golf course, increase the motivation of your teenager, facilitate greater levels of feedback on a work-team, understand organizational dynamics and their impact on human behavior, the construction of society to channel cultural energies, or for the ordering of consciousness itself, flow theory can provide valuable insights that give you new tools and strategies for navigating individual, team, organizational, and even societal experience. Clearly, what we've learned thus far about flow helps make sense of Hamilton's comment: "The ways we learn to entertain ourselves, to avoid boredom, or to cope with boredom have wide-spread personal, social, and ecological consequences."[9]

And finally, I'll quote Csikszentmihalyi again about why flow matters so much: "When a person's entire being is stretched in the full functioning of body and mind, whatever one does becomes worth doing for its own sake; living becomes its own justification. In the harmonious focusing on physical and psychic energy, life finally comes into its own."[10]

Developing the X Factor

As you begin your journey, it is important to make a distinction between the technical skills and the human performance skills.

Every Meaningful Life Arena (MLA) has its own set of Knowledge, Skills and Abilities (KSAs). For instance, in tennis there are approximately nine of these (serve, forehand, backhand, forehand approach shot, backhand approach shot, forehand volley, backhand volley, drop shot, overhead smash). For a PT boat captain the KSAs would be a bit more complex, but include advanced skills in navigation, seamanship, battle maneuvering, crew management, gun and missile deployment, and dozens of others. Very different arenas, tennis and patrolling, but as we discussed earlier there is something that draws these two things together; it's the ability to find flow in either arena.

While you consider your many MLAs, you will recognize that each arena requires unique technical skill sets. Your professional arena is quite different from your family arena, spiritual arena, social arena, etc. However, the skills that contribute to your flow are pervasive and apply to every arena that you engage in.

Taken together, the technical KSAs that comprise the foundation of each MLA, linked with the application of these flow strategies, gives you a distinct advantage over individuals who simply focus on their technical skills. Famed German tennis player Boris

Becker was once asked about his fifth set experience at Wimbledon. He commented that by the time anyone gets to the fifth and final set, it is no longer about the tennis. This is true for most high performers. There comes a time when, at a certain level, most everyone has the same basic technical competency levels, albeit different methods of delivery. After hitting a million forehands and backhands, conducting 2000 surgeries, assembling 5,000 cars, crowning 8,000 teeth, filing 10,000 tax returns, cooking 50,000 meals, or completing 2632 consecutive baseball games (a goal achieved by only one man: Cal Ripkin, Jr.), people develop expertise and proficiency in their craft. They meet and exceed that 10,000-hour mark where expertise is acquired.[11]

What can set us apart, then, is the study of peak performance and flow. Using appropriate strategies helps us fully engage ourselves, physically, emotionally, psychologically, philosophically, and spiritually. In combination with ongoing technical training, using these strategies for Finding Your Flow will make the difference in your current MLAs and any of your future MLAs, giving you the X Factor, or the special ingredients/competitive advantage that you have been looking for in your life.

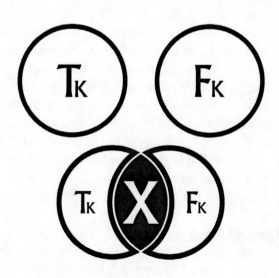

Tapping into this X-Factor means developing a completely new set of skills—skills that take your technical skills to the next level.

Flow: A Definition

Flow has many nuances, though nine[12] components have been described most often. Let's take a look at each:

1. <u>Clear Goals & Objectives</u>. When individuals describe their flow experiences during an activity, they often mention having a clear goal or "clear blueprint" of what to do.[13] Clear goals provide boundaries that help you channel your energy and focus on the objective at hand. Simultaneously, individuals in flow are often said to be "mindless." It is this duality, a combination of direction and detachment that helps bring about flow.

Perhaps one of the most thrilling goal-setting stories of the 20th century was the United States quest in the 1960s to land a man on the moon and return him safely to earth by the end of that decade. This goal was made public by a famous speech by John F. Kennedy after the Russians successfully launched Yuri Gagarin into space and back, and NASA then clarified its focus and unified its entire organization around this single goal. NASA folklore has it that late one night a senior director was walking the corridors of an office complex and saw what looked like an unauthorized man hovering about. When he inquired as to what this man was doing, the unknown figure stated, "Helping to put a man on the moon, sir!" He turned out to be the night janitor who was working late and making his own contribution towards the singularity of purpose that was NASA in the mid-1960s.

2. <u>Unambiguous/Immediate Feedback</u>. Feedback mechanisms are common to most natural and man-made systems.[14] They help monitor results, make adjustments, correct course, and re-direct

attention towards meaningful goals through measures and standards.[15] Thus, whether you make a poor golf shot, blow a sales call, or mess up on a professional presentation, the principle of feedback and your capacity for adjustment are vital to maintain your conscious attention and to move more efficiently towards your target. We need to learn from, adjust to, and re-engage with the many challenges of our lives that show up moment by moment. It is through feedback that all systems, be they simple (a thermostat) or complex (a human being) achieve their goals.

3. <u>Absence of Self-Consciousness</u>. Individuals who describe themselves in flow claim that they are "at one" with the experience. In contrast to individuals who are often being thrown to and fro within an experience, constantly thinking and wondering about what happened last time, what might happen this time, those who are in the midst of flow feel as if they are in the driver's seat. They react to every moment with relative ease.

While many individuals are ego-driven and consciously aware of themselves during any sort of performance, those finding their flow seem to let this go and experience the situation with a type of detachment. Who they are is no longer part of the equation. Neither fear of success nor fear of failure enters into the experience. Instead, the experience is what it is, without judgment, and the performer, almost as an observer, participates in this beautiful moment uninterrupted by the frailties of the human ego.

According to Duval and Wicklund,[16] individuals are either focused on themselves or on the environment. When focused on the self, individuals often judge themselves, and that takes their mind off the experience at hand and into their own heads, often creating negative feelings, self-comparisons, and other mental activities that usually end with poor focus and sub-par results.[17] Those who lack self-consciousness and stay in the moment, however, often feel at "their best selves".[18] They let their experience happen unhindered. Canadian Olympian Kim Alleston spoke of this:

For me it was a feeling of separating my body from my conscious mind and letting my body do what came naturally. When this happened things always went surprisingly well, almost as if my mind would look at what my body was doing and say, Hey, you're good. But at the same time not making any judgments on what I was doing because it was not "me" that was doing it; it was my body, and it was easy to stay in the present.[19]

4. Sense of Control. Individuals reporting flow experiences make comments such as, "I just couldn't miss the ball," or "Everything just came together." Such action and reaction patterns take place without much, if any, conscious processing. Individuals who attend to their current "reality"[20] or stay within the present moment[21] describe their ability to act spontaneously and without interference. I interviewed a male college basketball player (KM) who said, "I was ready to be where I needed to be, at the right place, and when I shot it was just like magic. Off my fingertips every time, every time I'd look at the basket I planned to make a shot. I had no doubt in my mind that I would make it."

5. Time Becomes Distorted. Individuals in flow often experience time going faster, especially during an enjoyable event. In my research, a female participant (BG) described how she had chosen a 700-page book she'd been meaning to read, and since her husband was gone for the day, she "sat down at about 8:30 in the morning and did not put the book down or move from that position until the book was done, 8 hours later."

The opposite phenomenon is also possible, where time seems to slow down. Michael Jordan once commented that at the end of a game, with only a few seconds left on the shot clock, that he had what seemed to be an unlimited amount of time to make the final basket— that the basketball got smaller while the hoop got bigger. He claimed to have all the time in the world as he knew

18

he could make the shot. Such was also the case with football great John Brodie who said:

> Sometimes time seems to slow way down, in an uncanny way, as if everyone were moving in slow motion. It seems as if I have all the time in the world to watch the receivers run their patterns, and yet I know the defensive line is coming at me just as fast as ever.[22]

6. Intrinsic Motivation. Researchers use the word *autotelic* for loving an experience for its own sake. Individuals in flow usually state that the experience brings them great joy and that there is no need for external rewards. They participate in certain activities "without conventional reward"[23] because they feel as if they are actualizing their potential. One female college student (BH) said, "I do not have the same desires I used to have to race. Now I just do it out of pure passion, for the activity itself, no other reason. I just do it 'cause I love it."

Essentially, individuals who find flow do so because they love what they do. An example: Ask yourself why Grandma likes to quilt or sew. Now try offering her cash for her quilts or blankets and notice the look on her face. What you've done is seek to replace her pure internal motives (sheer enjoyment of the process of sewing quilts) for an external one of minimal value to her (i.e., cold hard cash).

7. Centering of Attention. Your attention is constantly being pulled in many directions. Therefore it is difficult for your mind, whose normal condition is one of "informational disorder,"[24] to attend to a particular subject for any length of time. In order to enter flow, however, controlling your attention is a critical skill. It has been hypothesized that individuals with attention difficulties such as ADHD (Attention Deficit Hyperactivity Disorder) may be precluded from entering flow easily.[25] However, it is important to understand that attention issues are as much about context as ability. Both the intense reader and the

day-dreamer, one seemingly highly focused and the other wandering, may, in fact, be experiencing opposite kinds of flow.

8. <u>Merging of Action and Awareness (Transcendence)</u>. Merging action and awareness is essentially a fusion between body, heart, mind, spirit, and context. This fusion takes place when you're totally immersed in the task at hand and where even the tools you're using (bat, racket, piano, scalpel, computer) become part of you. In essence, "The unified consciousness brought about by the merging of action and awareness is perhaps the most telling aspect of the flow experience."[26] D.T. Suzuki had this to say about awareness and the sword master:

> If one really wishes to be master of an art, technical knowledge is not enough. One has to transcend technique so that the art grows out of the unconscious.... You must let the unconscious come forward. In such cases, you cease to be your own conscious master but become an instrument in the hands of the unknown. The unknown has no ego-consciousness and consequently no thought of winning the contest.... It is for this reason that the sword moves where it ought to move and makes the contest end victoriously.[27]

9. <u>Matching Skills and Challenge</u>. Flow takes place when the activity provides a context where your perceived challenges and your perceived skills meet.[28] Consider for a moment a time when you were given a task to do that seemed a bit boring—whether this was stacking cans in a grocery store, cleaning a floor, weeding a garden, or waiting around for someone. After a period of time, did boredom give way to anxiety or a desire to do something else? In contrast, think of a time when the challenge was over the top and you were not sure if you could manage it—a difficult exam perhaps, an overwhelming job, too many deadlines coming at you at once, multiple challenges, etc. Didn't this also lead to anxiety?

Flow occurs when you have the skill to complete a task, when you are confident that what you know combined with your past experience means "I can do this." The challenge may be a bit higher, where you aren't absolutely sure you can achieve your objective, but you think you have a good chance to pull it off. These are the experiences that teach you a little about yourself. They raise your confidence level and give you new insights into your capabilities.

CHAPTER 3: Experiencing Flow

Now let's get a bit deeper into how flow feels during an activity. Consider a skill like juggling. In essence, it provides a greater challenge than most people can navigate—at first. With three balls to contend with up front there might be an initial perception that the challenge is too great. Take away two of the balls and simply throw one ball up in the air, back and forth from hand to hand, and you have decreased the challenge significantly, making it very easy.

If you increase the challenge by introducing a second ball, you have made things more difficult but still doable with some instruction. You are told that with one ball in each hand, you must toss one ball up in the air towards the other hand, and after you see it at the top of its arc, you are to say the word "now" and at the same time toss the second ball from your other hand in a similar fashion. Now both balls are in the air and you are saying "now" each time a ball gets to the top of its arc. The one you tossed first falls into the opposite hand, while the ball you tossed second falls into the other opposite hand (both of which are free to catch a ball).

Ah, you realize that as long as you toss the ball each time the first ball gets to the top of its arc, that you always have a hand free to catch the ball just tossed. Now you understand the pattern. You toss both balls for a few minutes, calling "now" after each reaches the top of its arc, and now it seems easy. Your skills have now increased through light instruction and some practice.

After a while, tossing two balls gets to be a bit boring so you decide to add the third ball. With two balls in one hand and one ball in the other, you are reminded that as long as you toss into the air one ball from the hand holding two balls, wait until the first ball gets to the top of its arc, then toss the second ball from the other hand which will then be free to catch the first ball, and so on, that the juggling pattern just begins to take place, since there is always a ball in the air and one hand free to catch the next ball which is now falling from its arc.

As the pattern continues you recognize that your focus becomes more intense. You are tossing balls from each hand and saying "now" each time a ball reaches the top of its arc. You experience the rhythm with a toss "now" toss "now" toss "now" pattern, and you slowly become immersed in a deep moment of personal flow.[29]

As you can see with this brief experiment, you can produce flow with a combination of low challenge vs. low skill (an activity with few demands, such as sweeping a floor or folding clothes) or a combination of high challenge vs. high skill (such as doing your own taxes or flying the space shuttle). Any activity along the skills/challenge continuum provides an opportunity for that perfect balance that leads to flow.

Anything Can Be a Flow Arena

To better grasp flow, it's very helpful to listen to other people's experiences. The language they use reveals much about the inner workings of flow. Consider these very different activities:

Skiing

For me it was a feeling of separating my body from my conscious mind and letting my body do what came naturally. When this happened things always went surprisingly well, almost as if my mind would look at what my body was doing and say, hey, you're good. But at the same time not make any judgments on what I was doing because it was not "me" that was doing it; it was my body. This way, by not making any judgments, it was easy to stay in the present. (Canadian Olympian Kim Alleston) [30]

Bullfighting

All at once I forgot the public, the other bullfighters, myself, and even the bull; I began to fight as I had so often by myself at night in the corrals and pastures, as precisely as if I had been drawing a design on a blackboard. They say that my passes with the cape and my work with the muleta that afternoon were a revelation of the art of bullfighting. I don't know, and I'm not competent to judge. I simply fought as I believe one ought to fight, without a thought, outside of my own faith in what I was doing. With the last bull I succeeded for the first time in my life at delivering myself and my soul to the pure joy of fighting without being consciously aware of an audience. (Juan Belemonte, Spanish bullfighter [31])

Cross-Stitching

Friday afternoon, I was sitting there thinking that I would like to do something different. I got my pattern and material. I was thinking about the material and I kept going and going until midnight and my husband was like, "Aren't you going to bed?" and I was like, "What time is it?" And he said it was midnight. I was so into it that I forgot about the time; I was not conscious of anything around me. I just kept going. The next day I was so motivated, I did not even make breakfast and I did that for the whole day. I did not think about my husband; I just kept cross-stitching and when he came home I forgot to make dinner for him (SH, college student).

The Bosozuku Run

You are walking down the streets of Tokyo and to your astonishment you begin to hear the rumbling of 50 or more motorcycles. You watch as rowdy teenagers on wheels take over the roads, disrupt traffic, vandalize buildings, abuse citizens, and commit other types of dysfunctional activity. While everyone around you is in a state of panic, you notice that the young hellions seem to be enjoying themselves. What is it about their actions that is so attractive to them? Ikyua Sato studied this very

24

phenomenon, known as the "bosozuku run." Its participants describe it as enjoyable, full of play, an experience with clear rules, excitement, and other core components of the flow experience.

Sailing

Jim Macbeth explored the life of ocean cruising. Like any other powerful metaphor, sailing showcases the many components of flow. Prior to any voyage, the captain and crew chart a clear course (goals). Leisure or competition, the objective of the day is established. The boundaries, of course, are defined by the physical dimensions of the ship, but also in the clear rules and the roles as they are defined for each passenger. The natural obstacles provided by Mother Nature (wind, weather, waves) produce unique challenges and complexity that need to be addressed on a moment-to-moment basis. Each movement of the ship is assessed and compared to the course at hand. Navigation equipment (GPS/compass) provides instant feedback as to the progress of the vessel. As this symphony of behaviors evolves, the entire crew takes part in a complex web of experiences that trigger intrinsic enjoyment and excitement.

Surfing the Net and Gaming

The Internet is a place where many of us spend much of our time, and the engaging qualities of internet- and video-based gaming are well-known. Such games provide children and adults with all the aspects of flow, but without the physical exertion (excepting the Wii, of course). Web-site designers take special note of methods and strategies to draw attention and keep people on their sites. Like any other medium, games and internet resources command attention, provide clear boundaries, and offer challenges that keep us interested, motivated and focused. From virtual worlds (Second Life), staying connected (Facebook), buying and selling (eBay), to watching (YouTube), and so on, the world-wide web is an environment where flow is abundant.

Work

Many people describe flow in the context of their work. In fact, the work environment has been found to foster flow almost three times as often as leisure activities.[32]

One example: Susan, a sales representative from an upstart company, seeks to land her first big deal. Although fairly new with the company herself, she has an impressive track record. As one of the highest grossing salespeople, she is given the challenge to close the company's first million-dollar sale. In preparation, Susan visualizes the situation and identifies her main goals: to build rapport and trust with the vendor and to demonstrate the unique features of her company's product. While waiting in the front foyer, Susan takes a few deep breaths to calm her body, reminding herself of the dozen or so times she has previously made such a sale to other vendors. Her self-talk is positive. She believes without a doubt that this sale is already complete and she is merely here to close the deal. She confidently enters the vendor's office, and the sale is made precisely as she'd visualized it. And although it seemed to happen very quickly, she spent more than an hour in that office.

Religion

In addition to the transcendent possibilities of the more familiar Western religions, a number of Eastern cultural practices describe experiences similar to flow, from the "in the moment" behaviors of Japanese tea ceremonies to the oneness of the arrow and the target in archery.[33] Such practices and beliefs also include the idea of no practice, where entering new states of consciousness and oneness feature sitting in deep meditation or *Zazen*, Transcendental Meditation, and other types of passive practice.[34]

Everyday Experiences

Think about those ordinary activities that you get lost in, especially those where you find yourself so unconsciously competent that you no longer have to think about what you're doing: brushing your teeth, driving to work, crafting an email, discussing your company's product, filing documents. While these may not be the most exciting tasks, they do usher in automatic focus and patterns of behavior that need little conscious attention. Up the challenge just slightly on each of these tasks and you may find a narrowing of your attention and an increase in your engagement.

These examples parallel the observations of Buckingham and Coffman (in 1999) who noticed satisfied workers finding daily challenges through a proactive sense of personal mission and/or an ability to make use of internal strategies such as fantasy,[35] or interest regulation. [36] Such was the case with a team of housekeepers who had been cleaning rooms for a Disney hotel for more than two decades. In contrast to other workers who found themselves bored and unsatisfied, these Olympic-level cleaners discussed how they enjoyed the job by taking it to another level. Instead of just checking off the boxes when completing a certain chore, they looked for ways to improve their routine. From checking the ceiling for debris to re-arranging stuffed animals on the floor (if children were staying in the room), these super-performers were especially skilled at creating complexity and challenge in their everyday work.

This example may help us understand a new craze called "Extreme Ironing Around the World"—an international competition where individuals iron their clothes in unusual environments such as on a mountain, rafting down a river, or while scuba diving. As ridiculous as it sounds, this new sport beautifully demonstrates the value in applying flow theory, that is, taking the most simple of tasks and giving them unexpected twists.

While most of us do not think of cleaning hotel rooms or ironing clothes as extreme experiences, these examples reveal much about our ability to engineer our everyday environments. In contrast to the more typically engaging flow-worthy activities such as sailing, basketball, art, dance, flying, fighting fires, and so on, it is important to recognize that flow is no respecter of circumstance and can be found in almost any environment.

While some find flow in relatively few arenas, others enjoy glimpses of it everywhere. Even recognizing a single flow arena in your life will help you apply the principles and develop strategies for finding flow in other realms.

Do You Know What You Know?

We always begin an exploration at some level of ignorance, not knowing what we don't know. We then become aware enough to recognize the gap in our understanding, and then choose a new course or path to close that gap. Once a choice has been made, we then act upon that choice by seeking new knowledge, skills and experiences, which, over time, will develop into habits, perhaps even virtues. Again and again, we seek self-awareness and re-start the process, each time towards a new level.

Stephen R. Covey once commented, "Fish discover water last," meaning that we can be surrounded by something so much a part of us that we lack the ability to perceive it. A case in point: About 10 years ago a man living with his sister had become so obese that he could no longer leave the house, literally could not fit through the door. The day came when this man needed medical attention. Upon arrival, the police and fire crews had to break through the doorframe to remove the 1,000+ pound man. His caretaking sister reported that over the years she simply didn't notice that her brother had become so humongous. It was the removal of the door frame that gave it away. This was a shocking testament to the "boiled frog" syndrome, whereby placing a frog in boiling water will invoke a quick jumping response. However, leaving a frog in a warm pot of water and turning up the heat will cook the frog without its awareness.

Whether one suffers from obesity, neurotic tendencies, lack of focus, a poor self-image, bad breath, or any other unwanted

28

quality, behavior, habit or circumstance, self-awareness is the first step toward change.

One way to describe the process of personal change or self-mastery is to divide it into four phases:

1) Unconscious Incompetence—not knowing what you don't know, a gap in self-awareness or understanding;

2) Conscious Incompetence—knowing what you don't know, becoming self-aware and able to choose, or not, to make a change;

3) Conscious Competence—developing the skills to perform at a new level (i.e., learning how to write a personal mission statement, eat better, increase one's emotional intelligence, etc.); and once practiced, these skills are then integrated into one's being, generating habit patterns which develop into—

4) Unconscious Competence—giving you the ability to demonstrate any behavior with little conscious effort.

You demonstrate Unconscious Competence daily, when you brush your teeth, get dressed, drive to work, chew your food, push an elevator button, and so on. Each of these is an ingrained behavioral pattern that takes place without your conscious effort. When I describe this experience to seminar participants, most can relate to those days when they drove to work without any conscious awareness of how they did it. They enter the car, situate their gear for the day, turn on the radio, then poof! They simply "got to work." Their mind was somewhere else while their body managed to drive. I also refer to these moments as "mental macros" whereby we take multiple strings of actions, like a computer program does, by making one initial movement.

This is exciting, as it provides us a system for placing our attention on the critical aspects of our lives, and through time and practice, we can integrate new behavioral patterns that will establish new habits and routines. Before very long, living in these moments of unconscious competence begins to approximate this thing we call being in flow.

Looking Under the Hood of Your Ferrari

There's an analogy I like to use that may resonate with you. So many factors and mechanisms underlie flow that it can be compared to the functioning of a high performance machine.

In the late 1920s, Henry Ford declared that the Model T had more than 4,900 parts. That's a lot. Today, however, perhaps as many as ten times that number of parts contributes to a car's performance. Understanding the nature of flow is not unlike trying to understand the nature of any complex phenomenon or system. At first, looking under the hood and taking an engine apart can be quite a confusing challenge. Imagine popping the hood of a Ferrari and observing all of its impressive mechanics. You may notice a big engine block, a starter, cooling fans, hoses, wires, reservoirs for fluids, nuts and bolts and lots of other hardware.

But do many of us understand how each of these parts works together to generate the horsepower that propels this vehicle, let alone the many other features and systems that serve the driver? Most of us are happy to turn the key, press on the gas, and steer, while letting the mechanical marvel whiz us around.

What parts of this vehicle are actually, then, the most important? Surely you cannot drive this car without its steering wheel? It cannot move without all or most of its cylinders, nor can you accelerate without a gas pedal. Now what if you took off the glove compartment door? What if you removed the spare tire in the trunk, or the knob on the radio? While all of these parts contribute to the vehicle's total functioning, some parts are more essential than others.

Needless to say, all that complexity pales in comparison to that of the human body and mind. In fact, it pales in comparison to a common household fly. Nevertheless there is a principle here that cannot be ignored which suggests that some elements are more central than others. We might call these Vital Factors of performance. Consider the 80/20 principle: Under most circumstances, 80 per cent of one's efforts will produce roughly 20 per cent of the results, while at the same time about 20 per cent of one's efforts will produce 80 per cent of the results.

It's critical, then, to identify how to execute the behaviors that produce the greatest results in any situation. When it comes to finding your flow, what's needed is a systematic process of doing just that: identifying your own Vital Factors. You need a framework that allows you to look inside the complexity, observe it, then step back in order to notice how the pieces fit together. You need to be able to look under the hood (or into your life, in this case), observe a single part that adds a particular kind of value, then step back and see how that part contributes to your performance.

And shortly, in Sections II and III, we'll use this Ferrari analogy to dig deeper into *how* to make flow happen for you.

The Best of Times/The Worst of Times

Before we get to the nitty gritty of detailed strategies, let's spend a short time doing a bit of qualitative research. We'll use grounded theory, as that's the best way to delve usefully into your own flow experiences. Let me take a moment to explain.

The two great families of research are quantitative (things we can count) and qualitative (an essence or quality of a scientific phenomenon, something you seek to describe). Often, the qualitative (observing) comes first and the quantitative (counting) comes second.

Within the qualitative realm, one method of discovery is known as grounded theory. In essence, this method suggests that you, as the principle investigator (of your own experience, in this case), want to observe something of value and to notice what emerges within the course of your experience. As you start to observe and collect data from this experience, themes emerge. You may begin to notice that each time you have performed poorly, for example, you were focused on what others were thinking about you. Or you'll discover that when you take time in the morning to plan out your day, you're much more efficient and zip through your task list. Perhaps you'll recognize that whenever you manage less than six hours of sleep your mood is somewhat off-kilter. With enough data gathered, you can begin to draw conclusions about the frequency of a given phenomenon.

Now let's consider two contrasting sets of experience. To begin, review the phrases below, and for each, ponder a time when something like it happened to you:

- You were overwhelmed with your work or life
- You lacked interest in what you were doing
- What you were doing had little or no value to you
- Time stood agonizingly still

- You felt a sense of frustration or fear
- You were not on purpose
- There was a disconnect between your mind, heart, and body
- You were overly self-conscious
- There was a sense of self-doubt
- You were impatient to do something other than what you were doing

Did one or more experiences come to mind? When speaking with workshop participants, I find that there is an almost unlimited number of experiences that generate such responses: being stuck in a boring, routine, or uninspiring job; a relationship going bad; freezing up during an important test; being in a broken-down boat in the middle of the lake; speaking in front of a large audience; finding yourself stuck at a family reunion listening to the same old stories. Such frustrating experiences can be labeled "anti-flow." Take a moment and write down, in as much detail as you can, times you experienced "anti-flow."

Times when I was in anti-flow:

1. _____
   _____
   _____
   _____
   _____
   _____
   _____
   _____

2. _____
   _____
   _____
   _____
   _____
   _____
   _____

3. _____
   _____
   _____
   _____
   _____
   _____
   _____
   _____
   _____

4. _____
   _____
   _____
   _____
   _____
   _____
   _____
   _____

5. _____
   _____
   _____
   _____
   _____
   _____
   _____
   _____

Now let's consider the opposite. Take some time to reflect upon exceptionally positive and joyous experiences. These are times when:

- Your mind wasn't wandering
- You were not thinking of something else
- You were totally involved and absorbed in what you were doing
- Your body, heart, mind and spirit were completely engaged
- Nothing seemed to bother or get at you

- You were less aware of your problems and yourself
- The stars seemed to align and everything just fell into place
- You seemed to have all of the skills you needed to do the job
- You were in complete control of the situation
- You felt highly energized to be doing what you were doing
- You didn't see yourself as separate from what you were doing
- Time seemed to fly by
- You and your activity were one

Times when I was in flow:

1. _____
   _____
   _____
   _____
   _____
   _____
   _____
   _____

2. _____
   _____
   _____
   _____
   _____
   _____
   _____
   _____

3. _____

_____

_____

_____

_____

_____

_____

_____

4. _____

_____

_____

_____

_____

_____

_____

5. _____

_____

_____

_____

_____

_____

_____

If you were to ask athletes, lawyers, doctors, teachers, salespeople, parents—you name a group—about when they had flow experiences, where do you think they described them taking place? You might have guessed it: in relationships, taking a test, fixing a broken boat, speaking in front of a large group, and yes—even at family reunions. Both exceptionally negative as well as exceptionally positive experiences can stem from the same places and activities.

Now, it's time to go deeper into yourself and your experience.

SECTION II – Flow Strategies Overview

CHAPTER 4: External Strategies

Flow strategies—specific ways to help you enter a highly engaged, highly focused flow state—can be divided into many categories. After the overview in this chapter, we will then dig deeper in the next chapter and begin the process of assessing your own Flow Assets and Liabilities.

Flow strategies can be broken into three main categories: External Strategies, Internal Strategies, and Time-Based Strategies. Beneath these three themes, there are eleven sub-categories, which then reveal the more than 150 more specific strategies that you can use to find your flow. But don't worry—you don't need to memorize a thing. You're simply going to assemble a vast arsenal of tools you can resort to when flow doesn't come easily.

Think of it this way: As you look under the hood of your Ferrari, you will be taking apart the vehicle (i.e., yourself) in sections. The engine (or mind) is the largest section, followed by the drive train, doors, external body parts, interior parts, and so on. Then you will put all related parts together in their respective piles or themes. If you have ever tried to take something mechanical apart and then tried to put it back together again without instructions, you know the value of keeping all the parts in their separate piles. And yet, there always seems to be extra parts. Having a broad perspective of key flow themes and strategies can be quite helpful in seeing how each part relates to the others while at the same time showcasing its singular value.

Be aware that each theme touched on below is its own science with hundreds of studies and books written on each. The descriptions below simply scratch the surface, but see if you can locate them in your own life and notice how each may be playing a role in your own ability to enter a state of flow.

Finding flow is about preparing, managing, and cultivating your experiences, either from the outside (external strategies) or on the inside (internal strategies). In this chapter, we'll start with the external.

Choosing the Right Environment

Being in an environment that provides new challenges, insights or feelings of peace, can by itself induce flow. Often such a favorite place, by your simply showing up, makes you feel at home or at peace with the world.

JP, a high school student, had this to say about tapping into flow by stepping into her favorite environment:

> My place is Sundance [Utah]. I love it there and that is where I feel at peace and am one with nature—when I am somewhere safe. . . . When I'm at school I am pretty shy and it is hard for me to get out to people but when I am up at Sundance or somewhere in the mountains I am totally myself, and I have complete confidence in who I am. I think it is a safety issue with where you are. I found it just by experience, just by being up there.

For many, a natural place brings out their focus. It allows them to get away from the artificial and allows them to lose themselves in a more natural order. For DR, a college senior, this was a major strategy:

> I think flow is a state where you can really kind of lose yourself; that is why I think nature is so key. A lot of times, if I am writing or doing something,

I want to get out of the house, even if my room is ordered or whatever. I have to focus more to get into flow, when I am outside it is easier for me to get into that kind of flow when I am writing or whatever. I think it is the feeling of getting away from all of that stuff, where you can lose yourself in that environment.

For others, the right man-made environment works well. A dance studio, a surgical theater, or a garden—such places are pre-organized by their very nature to help focus your attention.

Some speak about the value of finding a quiet or isolated place, choosing the right time to enter a certain place, a place that's safe, or a place so naturally appealing that being there makes one happy and focused in the moment. For RC, an experienced medical researcher, isolation is key:

One of the strategies I use is basically isolation, where I separate myself from other people and activities that may be going on around me. I will just remove myself physically from that setting to one where I can focus on what I really want to do, whether it be gardening or being outside by myself, listening to music or reading a book.

Considering the many spaces in your life, do you have a certain space or place that invites the flow experience? Is it an office, a reading room, the pool at the gym, in your car? Perhaps it is a natural space: the local park, a garden, or your own back yard. Begin noticing the spaces in your life where flow seems to await your arrival.

Regulating the Environment

While some people get into flow merely by entering a certain space, many of us find our flow only when we have engineered that space to make it more conducive to our particular needs.

Think of a massage room or a spa. Look at all of the variables they control, such as sound (with natural music), light (usually low light), heat (usually slightly warmer), and smell (some type of incense or aroma). Put these variables together with a good masseuse and you find yourself focused totally in the moment of the massage.

Consider your nightly bed-time rituals. Do you make sure that the temperature is just right? Do you have a system for getting the right amount of sheet and blanket to cover you? Do you manipulate your pillow in just the right way? What about your physical position? Think of the little things taken together that you do to initiate the right conditions for optimal sleep.

A young college student (BG) describes how she readies herself and her environment to read a book that she was waiting to devour.

> First I have to make myself comfortable, I have to make the room comfortable, whether that is finding the right position on the couch or on the bed, getting enough pillows and blankets. I kind of work from the inside out. You kind of set the book there and light some candles or put on music or something like that. As soon as I am comfortable I stop fiddling with my environment and get down to business. The process of getting the room ready and getting to relax, getting ready to read is a big part of getting into it.

I once interviewed a divorce mediation attorney who was quite successful at facilitating troubled relationships. Describing what she did differently from other divorce lawyers, she said that her first order of business was to conduct all of her mediation sessions in her own living room. When facilitating what was a very emotionally charged event, it was counter-productive to be in an office where everything was straight business. Instead, being in a living room was more like home and produced a much more comfortable and open atmosphere.

This mediator then went on to discuss the many other controllable variables of the house such as the lights, the temperature, how the chairs were positioned, the colors of the drapes, etc. "And we [my clients and I] are in a circle, which is really important. No tables. When I mediated out of a law office, I did not have flow like I do in a home environment."

This clever attorney figured out what kind of environment she needed to lighten the mood, channel the communication, and help each person focus on the issues at hand. Other environmental regulation strategies may include the use of art or the placement of inspirational messages, removing anything that produces a distraction (including taking the phone off the hook if necessary), and creating boundaries which allow the person to focus more intently on what is most important.

Perhaps there is more you could do to tweak and tune one or more of your current environments. These are a few of the questions that you will be asked to consider as you take the Finding Your Flow Self Analysis later in this book.

Interpersonal Regulation

Accessing a flow state may also have much to do with how you relate to other people. Friends, colleagues, and family members help us by being supportive, giving us feedback, taking on certain burdens, or playing roles that help us stay focused.

A pediatric doctor explained how her administrative staff assisted her focus and flow by keeping her medical charts organized and placing them next to the door of each patient that she was about to see. This simple strategy allowed her to keep her mind on what was most important (the patient) in order to stay focused in the moment and not on administrative tasks. Of course, this is what assistants do: They support us in our daily work. They relieve certain burdens that allow us to stay focused on the tasks at hand.

When I speak with people about their interpersonal flow experiences, some mention the importance of choosing the right people and of building synergy with others. According to one experienced female participant (DW) in a workshop:

> I certainly could lose myself in that it was a wonderful experience. There is sort of a human connection going on which is much more profound than ordinary. And while touching people's lives, it seems like I could lose myself in that.

One female high school student discussed synergy in both dancing and theater:

> In ballroom, if your partner knows what he is doing, it makes it more fun and you just want to keep doing it until your time is up. In drama, when people know their lines or you have a set plan of what you are going to do, it helps everything flow together.

Another college student (SG) discussed his connection to his audience while playing music:

> Either they are engaging, or they are getting charged. For example, they are having an emotional connection with our music; it can almost bring them to tears, and when I can see that it has a physical effect on those people, that's when flow happens for me.

Still others find flow by hanging out with friends: "Even when I just hang out with people that like to do the same thing, it just keeps it going. We have the same flow and they help increase it." Some describe flow as synergizing around a deep conversation. According to a male attorney:

Sometimes you are interacting with someone and your mind just clicks with what they are talking about. Things just start clicking and you reach that certain high or zone, whether it is work or a social deal.

Being affirmed or validated often helps people find their flow. In one case, a workshop participant described being affirmed by another individual which boosted his confidence. However, many people have positive feelings—even feelings of flow—when supporting or affirming others. The latter moves you beyond yourself to focus on another person's needs. SW compared sportsmanship with affirming others:

> Sportsmanship is basically an affirmation of relationship between people. We are all interrelated, and anything that elevates this relatedness is going to end up freeing us.

A high school student felt a similar need to affirm others:

> Before I start to get into flow, I like to compliment one other player on the team because I know that it helps them out and it helps me out. It just makes everyone happier and makes us think about the game.

In essence, affirming others, even showing respect for others, is a strategy that generates certain internal feelings as well as affecting external conditions that change the mood and nature of the situation, removing pressure and offering a more conducive space for flow to take place.

Still others find a sense of interpersonal flow while teaching a class, reading a letter and feeling very connected to the person who wrote it, walking with friends in the mountains, or dancing with others. BC, a male professional educator, stated: "There is something that happens on a group level that propels flow because you are communicating on the same wavelength."

Because other people play vital roles in our many Meaningful Life Arenas, we must become aware of how they contribute to or hinder our ability to find our flow.

In the next chapter, we'll look at some of the internal strategies used in achieving a flow state.

CHAPTER 5: Internal Strategies

We'll begin this round-up of internal strategies with a discussion of spiritual methods used by those seeking to enter flow. As throughout this book, feel free to adapt what you read to suit your own temperament and belief system.

Spiritual Strategies

For many, finding flow begins with the understanding that being in the moment is predicated on the understanding that we live in a world governed by a higher power—one that we have the opportunity to tap into. To do this requires faith, humility, non-judgment, recognizing the divine nature of things, prayer, feeling the spirit, studying scriptures or spiritual works, tapping into one's deepest values, and/or having a vision of one's inherent potential.

Such individuals feel compelled to ask themselves: "How can flow find me instead of me finding it?" Instead of seeking to control everything in a highly complex and changing world, many people find that learning to think, feel, and behave in concert with their idea of a God or a higher power helps them tap into greater sources of energy and focus. SG, a male college senior, explained:

> That is a huge element for me, connecting with myself, having that spiritual connection. I do not care if I am physically on, mentally on, if I do not have the connection with the cosmos. If I were to rank all of those areas, physical, mental, social, emotional, and spiritual, I can be in harmony in those three dimensions. But if I am out of it spiritually, I cannot make it happen.

RJ, an attorney, discussed the value of tapping into the spiritual aspects of self:

> I think it comes to people that have a spiritual background, regardless of what age, religion, nationality; having some kind of belief or basis for their life enhances their performance and their feeling of well-being and probably self-esteem.

Many spoke about the power of prayer in inducing flow. One male college senior (SG) commented, "I like to go to the mountains. I like to pray. A combination of those things helps me engage in the concept of flow."

Another male college student (DR) expanded on the value of prayer, showing that it can be used as a meta-strategy for tapping into other strategies:

> Prayer for me is the basis of everything. It allows you to lose yourself, it allows you to be calm, it allows you to focus, it allows you to prepare yourself to where you can start building up, where you can start visualizing, you can start all that preparatory stuff to where you can get into flow.

Prayer is a strategy often used by those about to deal with difficult problems or seemingly unsolvable issues. An experienced male doctor said, "If I am expecting a problem, I feel like prayer is helpful." Similarly, a female attorney (LB) stated,

> I always pray before a coaching session. I think with a prayer, it opens up my attitude, the willingness to be receptive to whatever comes, and it just releases you.

One male college student (DR) said, "I enter flow through prayer and scripture study and through contemplating and meditating. I do not do it a lot but I will tell you when I do, I really feel that it is very valuable."

Overall, prayer is a strategy that seems to tap into a variety of other strategies, helping individuals reach a higher source of power, feel a sense of confidence and/or peace, and recognize that seeking answers beyond oneself can be an important step for finding flow.

Learning to let go is a spiritual strategy many people mention to me. Comments like "letting it happen" or "freeing it up" are often used as a more abstract way for inviting flow to take place. Letting go is often referred to in a spiritual sense of faith, freeing the mind and letting go of the moment or letting go of one's insecurities. One female college senior (HK) discussed how she kept flow going once it started:

> Just not letting things bother me, keeping up a positive attitude, keep the faith is a way to it, deciding not to allow things to interfere with my plans and my dreams and letting go of things that I cannot control.

After I reviewed the comments of those who used spiritual strategies, a key issue turned out to be learning to recognize what one could or could not control. Individuals that described this letting-go process often did not have a particular way of doing this. Rather it was a notion they kept in mind, offering them an opportunity to release all extraneous details and focus on the present task. An older very experienced female summarized this nicely: "I do not do a lot of analyzing. I might recognize flow but I do not pick it apart. It is kind of like pulling the wings off a butterfly."

Still others speak of the importance of humility, of believing that flow is a gift from a higher source and not necessarily from anything that we do. Tapping into and submitting oneself to this power can be crucial. BC, a male professor, expressed his view this way:

> There has to be also a spiritual dimension to my flow, in a sense of humility. While there is a great sense of confidence in the process, I attribute that knowledge and the type of flow as not necessarily being from me.

Some speak about their spiritual selves within the context of connecting other parts of self. One male college student (SG) had this to say about the holistic nature of flow:

> For me there is an intersection, there is a balance between my four dimensions of life. There is a balance between my physical, mental, spiritual, and emotional self. It seems to me what is happening in my life before I experience flow is that there is a harmony between those four dimensions. My personal life is going well. Academically, things are going well. Also physically, I am taking care of my body, socially, emotionally, the relationships that I am having with other people, and spiritually. So whether it is playing music or sports, if those four dimensions are in sync, that is when I experience flow.

Philosophical Strategies

Sometimes mingling with spiritual strategies but somewhat different and very personal, philosophical strategies can be used to tap into values that can help support focus and intent. Through years of studying great men and women, I have discovered that in addition to their spiritual foundation or their relationship with a higher power, many of them have also declared a personal philosophy. It's what I call a Philosophy of Engagement, and this is what guides them along their daily journey. Some talk about their philosophy by declaring core beliefs and principles.

Abraham Lincoln's personal creed focuses mostly on his belief in a higher power quoted in detail here:

> I believe in God, the Almighty Ruler of Nations, our great and good and merciful Maker, our Father in heaven, who notes the fall of a sparrow, and numbers the hairs of our heads.

> I believe in His eternal truth and justice. I recognize the sublime truth announced in the Holy Scriptures and proven by all history that those nations only are blest whose God is the Lord.

> I believe that it is the duty of nations as well as of men to own their dependence upon the overruling power of God, and to invoke the influence of His Holy Spirit; to confess their sins and transgressions in humble sorrow, yet with assured hope that genuine repentance will lead to mercy and pardon.

> I believe that it is meet and right to recognize and confess the presence of the Almighty Father equally in our triumphs and in those sorrows which we may justly fear are a punishment inflicted upon us for our presumptuous sins to the needful end of our reformation.

> I believe that the Bible is the best gift, which God has ever given to men. All the good from the Saviour of the world is communicated to us through this book.

> I believe the will of God prevails. Without Him all human reliance is vain. Without the assistance of His divine Being, I cannot succeed. With that assistance I cannot fail.

Being a humble instrument in the hands of our Heavenly Father, I desire that all my works and acts may be according to His will; and that it may be so, I give thanks to the Almighty, and seek His aid.

I have a solemn oath registered in heaven to finish the work I am in, in full view of my responsibility to my God, with malice toward none; with charity for all; with firmness in the right as God gives me to see the right. Commending those who love me to His care, as I hope in their prayers they will commend me, I look through the help of God to a joyous meeting with many loved ones gone before.

Others express their Philosophy of Engagement by describing more personal attitudes and perspectives outside of standard spiritual ideals. Thomas Dekker, the Elizabethan poet and dramatist, described his philosophy this way:

To awaken each morning with a smile brightening my face;

To greet the day with reverence for the opportunities it contains;

To approach my work with a clean mind;

To hold ever before me, even in the doing of little things, the Ultimate Purpose toward which I am working;

To meet men and women with laughter on my lips and love in my heart;

To be gentle, kind, and courteous through all the hours;

To approach the night with weariness that ever
woos sleep, and the joy that

Comes from work well done –

This is how I desire to waste wisely my days.

Still others discuss the qualities and virtues of greatness in their
Philosophy of Engagement. Poet Howard Arnold Walter
declared:

I would be true, for there are those who trust me:

I would be pure, for there are those who care:

I would be strong, for there is much to suffer.

I would be brave, for there is much to dare.

I would be friend to all—the foe, the friendless:

I would be giving, and forget the gift.

I would be humble, for I know my weakness:

I would look up—and laugh—and love—and lift.

Thomas Jefferson declared the rules and standards that he
espoused to live by in his Decalogue, which read:

1.   Never put off till tomorrow what you can
     do today.

2.   Never trouble another for what you can do
     yourself.

3.   Never spend your money before you have it.

4.   Never buy what you do not want, because it is cheap: it will be dear to you.

5.   Pride costs us more than hunger, thirst, and cold.

6.   We have never repented of having eaten too little.

7.   Nothing is troublesome that we do willingly.

8.   How much pain has cost us the evils which never happened.

9.   Take things always by their smooth handle.

10.   When angry, count ten, before you speak: if very angry, an hundred.

By offering guidelines for living their core ideals, such personal philosophies allow people yet another avenue (in contrast to strictly spiritual ideals) to solidify values and to ground personal thought patterns and behaviors. This channels their energy and keeps them focused on what is most important in life, and that, in turn, can feed into flow.

Psychological Strategies

Motivation

With countless motivational theories seeking to explain human behavior, there is a clear distinction between those outside forces that prompt us to act (extrinsic motives) and those inside motives that emanate from our very core (intrinsic motives). Another way to look at motivational theories is through the lens of pleasure and pain to better understand what drives our behavior.

External motives may include such things as receiving positive or negative feedback, the feeling you get when you do something for others, or external rewards such as money, recognition, and other benefits you enjoy from the world around you.

By contrast, most people who enter flow easily find they have a more powerful friend with intrinsic motivation. There are certain things you do for their own sake, and the activity itself is so enjoyable that there is no need for external rewards. Such is the case with avid golfers, mountain climbers, readers, and so on. Almost anything that you enjoy doing without considering outcome or external reward can help you tap into flow.

As we look at these different types of motives, we might consider the contrast between pleasure and pain or positive and negative. In general terms we seek to avoid pain (physical, emotional, psychological, etc.) while seeking to move towards pleasure (happiness, contentment, positive feelings, etc.). In many cases negative motives are quite effective. We may be motivated to stay away from someone we don't like, or a hot stove, or from annoying the IRS. These are powerful motives but they do not usually connect us to our peak states of flow. By contrast, positive motives attract us and we seek them out.

By putting these two continuums together, we get four distinct quadrants: Extrinsic/Pain (usually based on fear, often triggering a fight or flight response); Intrinsic/Pain (internal feeling states that you wish to stay away from, such as self-doubt, fear, or anxiety); Extrinsic/Pleasure (motives such as money, fame, objects that you desire); and Intrinsic/Pleasure (motives that tap into your best self, that give you innate joy and pleasure). This shift, from extrinsic rewards or pleasure to intrinsic rewards and pleasure is an important shift for most people. Making the shift often helps individuals tap into new sources of energy and enjoyment that run deeper and lead to a more profound sense of self. A retired female professor (JV) commented:

> Certainly I am more likely to have a flow experience when the activity I am engaged in gives me pleasure. . . . If I were to have a strategy it would be to go do what I feel like doing.

Taking motivational theory to another level, consider those activities that tap into your highest values, such as those that transcend self-interest, that push you and stretch you and perhaps serve a higher purpose. Here is where you are making use of energy that is well beyond the mere physical. Rather, you are connecting with your philosophical, even your spiritual, self. For some this is serving their God or a higher power. For others it is dedicating themselves to a cause such as an AIDS walk, a medical mission, or serving as an ecclesiastical leader in a church. Wherever such key motivational sources originate, they can help you tap into flow.

Visualization

The quintessential strategy of high performers is visualization: using the mind's eye to see, plan, practice, execute, review, and repeat excellent performances.

In the world of sport and performance psychology, the skill of visualizing is as important as being able to run well or lift weights. No matter what the arena, through visualization you can pre-plan your strategies, practice your performance either by seeing yourself achieving your objective from the inside out, or from the outside in, observing yourself from afar. You can take more risk in your mind, play around with various strategies, and even try things you are not yet comfortable doing in real life.

Visualization has been used for thousands of years. Early accounts of mental training can be traced back to Buddhist monks trekking from India to China. On their way they were often the victims of theft and barbarism until they learned to fight with hands and feet, thus inventing the martial arts. One of their chief strategies was visualization. This allowed them to train and practice at any place or any time.

A case in point is this male college senior (PA) preparing for his sporting activities:

> Usually I step back from where I'm actually going to be performing. I take a couple steps back on the golf course. I'll look straight down the fairway where I want it to be, and then picture myself swinging the golf club and picture the ball actually going straight down the middle. . . . In basketball, shooting free throws even before I bounce the ball, I stand there a second and picture the shot going in before I get up and go through it.

College student KM discusses his process of visualization, which includes deep breathing, progressive muscle relaxation, and other ways of self-calming:

> When I go into situations, I'm really trying to focus on things. I think about my breathing patterns, in the nose, out the mouth, and picturing actually doing the task at hand—fulfilling it. Performing it to the ability that I want in my head. So I see it all the way through, from A to Z, exactly how I want to do it or how it needs to be done.

Another college student (AM) discusses the value of visualization before a competitive event. She describes both visualizing from the inside and from the outside:

> The first is in order to recreate the flow experience. A couple days before the event I will lie down very calmly and picture the situation that I will be in and try to be in the situation, as far as the smell of the pool and the sound of the crowd. It's really important that nothing in the situation is

different for me. I try to imagine a certain time or a goal and watch myself do it, kind of like I am watching from the stand at the beginning, and then going through and actually doing it, what the water feels like and the taste of water in your mouth, looking up at the scoreboard and seeing the results.

Visualization is useful beyond the athletic arena. An experienced educator, BS, for example, describes his use of this strategy:

Seeing yourself involved in your class, reformatting what you have prepared and used previously. In a sense, you are kind of role-playing or thinking of yourself in the classroom. In that kind of lesson preparation, I experience a great deal of high-level concentration.

WM, also an educator, had this to say about preparing for an art project:

In the art domain, in welding, I may have cogitated on a piece in my head or maybe in scratches for a long time before I put it in the material. I may have worked it over and over and over again so that it is deeply into my head.

Goal-Setting

Probably the most common human performance strategy in the world is the setting of goals. Goal-setting is used to channel energy, focus attention, and hold yourself accountable for results. Researchers have found that although less than three per cent of the world's population have *written* goals, these individuals out-earn the standard population by more than 10 times.[37]

One review of goal-setting studies showed that over 91% showed positive results, which represents a performance increase of between 8.4% and 16%.[38] Another comprehensive review shows the generalizability of goal-setting studies "across different tasks, settings, performance criteria, and types of subject"[39] and other analyses.[40] Simply stated, goal setting is a strategy the works for just about everyone who does it.

Goal-setting, from short-term to long-term, written or non-written, provides structure. It channels energy in a particular direction by translating strategic intentions into focused action.

In the early 1960s John F. Kennedy declared to the American people, "We choose to go to the moon, because that goal will help to organize and measure the best of our energies and skills." After Martin Luther King, Jr., declared "I have a dream," this vision of the future of American values was then broken down into clear goals and objectives that would move the U.S. closer to his ideals. No company or organization can function without articulating specific goals and objectives. And whether you think about it consciously or not, each of us sets goals on a daily, even hourly, basis as goals, written or not, drive our behavior every day.

Goals come in many forms. Some focus on outcome, others on the process. Still other goals focus neither on outcome nor process but instead help us compete against our own performance standards. Long-term goals look further into the future while intermediate and short-term goals focus our attention more closely in the present moment.

As we consider the power of goal-setting, we must also consider the value of balance. Goal-setting may include physical, career, family, personal, spiritual, and any other life category that balances out your life equation. Using techniques such as ranking goals by time, value, and life arena, including the use of SMART (making goals Specific, Meaningful/Measurable, Aggressive yet Realistic, and Time-driven) helps you organize and marshal your personal energies, serving to keep your intentions and values firmly set in the moment.

Thought and Self-Talk

Another important psychological strategy makes use of internal thoughts or self-talk. Self-talk assists people in modifying their moods, increasing self-confidence, prolonging persistence, modifying self-image, and helping to accomplish other modes of performance enhancement.

As you are aware, most of our internal climate is filled with thinking. Fill your mind with negative thoughts and you will find your emotions running out of control. This is why almost every book on personal development or performance enhancement includes a chapter or two on managing your thoughts. Similarly, great performers who successfully find their flow are excellent at managing their internal dialogue. Negative thinkers struggle more with focus than positive thinkers. Essentially they are distracted by their inner voice—the dialogue that rolls around in their head while they are trying to focus in the moment works against them.

In the words of one male college senior:

> I use my positive self-talk to try to generate confidence. It works out the negative thoughts. . . . I try to keep myself motivated and keep myself confident. When I'm starting to think, "Don't screw this up," or "Don't mess up," I try to really force that out of my head as soon as possible and get back to, "OK, you can do this. You've done this many times. You can do it again."

Another male college senior (DR) explains how he uses self-talk in combination with other strategies:

> I think you use some of these other strategies, you focus on different events, you visualize, you breath differently as if you were in the event, and you feel the emotion of it especially, and you build them; you

mentally create an energy, even if it's just "I can do this, I can do this. I am going to do it. I am the best, I am the best." Not in a real prideful way, but there are thoughts like, "I can succeed, I can succeed!" building up this positive energy and the feelings and emotions of it that really heighten your power.

Critical to the value of self-talk is the recognition that what you say to yourself—even your feelings or attitudes— is under your control. SW, a male athlete, professor and coach, states, "I am continually reminding myself and others that it is my attitude that I am focusing on, my choice to be positive with regard to everything that happens."

For another example, an elderly professional (SS) uses self-talk to review and rehearse future events, similar in strategy to mental rehearsal: "I give myself a pep talk to begin with, knowing that it is going to be demanding whatever it is, so I tell myself what is ahead of me, I tell myself about the experience, I tell myself about the rewards. I rehearse all of that in my mind."

Nobody is immune to inner interference. Consider a vital performance that you recently experienced. Where you afraid, nervous, excited? You can associate certain feelings with certain thoughts: "You can do it"; "What will happen if I screw this up?"; "I've never done this before." Your inner voice is capable of playing either the advocate or the critic and can have a profound effect on how well you do.

Individuals who learn to use this inner voice, or have trained themselves to shut off their thinking and let their experiences take place without judgment, are able to focus even more intently in the moment. As thought governs attention, it is easy to see that learning to control the mind is the gateway for controlling everything else.

Filtering and Locus of Control

Being in flow requires filtering out unwanted information and controlling the controllable. To do this, we must learn to ignore others, time, problems, pressures, outcomes, sometimes ourselves, even the activity we are in if we are to let it happen automatically. Those who have mastered focus recognize the power of letting go and paying attention only to those aspects that are relevant to the situation at hand.

SW, a world-class athlete and coach, comments:

> It is really important that there is a clear distinction between the things that are within your control and outside your control and that you stay focused on what you have control over and that you hang loose on the things that are not.

Many people get caught up in trying to filter out irrelevant things only to find that they are thinking about (or seeking to control) the actual things they are trying to ignore (the score, fear, self-doubt, what others are thinking, and so on).

Basketball great John Wooden once posited this riddle: "You have only a few seconds left on the shot clock. Who do you throw the ball to: The person who is thinking about winning, the person who is afraid of losing, or the person who is focused on taking the shot?" Of course, the answer is number three. These questions reveal just how much we get caught up in the moment and let irrelevant thoughts and feelings get in the way of paying attention to what matters most. Ultimately these are issues of control (or perceived control). We are constantly navigating what we can control, what we can't control, and what we are seeking to control.

Here is HK, a female college student, on the importance of recognizing what she can and cannot control:

I have to sit down and say, "Okay, this is what has been messing me up, I do not have control over this so I am not going to worry about it." This is more like a process; I have to say it over and over again. If I start thinking about something, I have to tell myself that I am not going to think about that, I do not have control over that. I do not have control over whatever it is and let it go.

Perspective

As we gather experiences in life, it is often customary to put these experiences in little boxes to define them. "This was a good experience," "This was a bad experience," "Why did this happen to me?" and so on. If you study the accounts of individuals who have gone through significant struggles, such as surviving concentration camps, you find that managing their perspective was a core strategy for staying in the moment and for coping— some even flourishing—with the incredible challenges.

You don't hear about this skill as much as the others, but it is indispensible. You might liken it to mental flexibility or the ability to look at any issue, problem, or circumstance from a variety of angles. This offers you an ever increasing number of opportunities to think, emote, and behave in ways that are healthy and more productive. Think of a circle with an unlimited number of arrows pointing towards it. Each arrow is pointing at the same object, but each aims at or illuminates a different part of it.

The Hindus have discussed the idea of perspective for hundreds of years. Consider for a moment the parable of the blind men and the elephant:

There were six blind men trying to explain what an elephant is like. One of the men was standing against the animal and suggested that it was just like a wall. Another man was holding on to the elephant's tusk and declared it was much like a spear. A third man was holding onto its trunk and explained that the creature was much like a snake. The forth man was feeling the animal's knee and declared that it was much like a tree. The fifth man, holding its ear, explained that it was more like a fan. Finally the sixth blind man, holding the elephant's tail, explained that in fact the animal was more like a rope.

The six men argued because each was clear that his data was the most correct. Each man sought to express his understanding from his own vantage point, only to recognize finally that he had only understood a small part of the whole animal.

This is a powerful illustration of what it means to illuminate truth and how each of us is limited in our ability to see an entire picture. As you consider the issues in your own life, recognize that you may only be seeing through a very small window. Recognize that with a little mental flexibility and angle-seeking, a more productive perspective is available to you. In pursuing flow, you may need to access a broader perspective at times and then move towards a more limited perspective. Perhaps some humor is needed to manage the struggle of the moment. In making sense of why an event happened, you may choose a long-term perspective, even a spiritual perspective. Choosing from a variety of perspectives gives you much-needed flexibility.

A professional attorney (RJ) referenced perspective when speaking about the importance of his family when making life decisions: "When doing the right things for yourself, for your family, for others, I look for the bigger picture."

A fuller example comes from psychologist and attorney Christopher R. Barden. His story:

> Nine years of training in clinical psychology, four years of training in the martial arts, and several years as a tennis professional had, I thought, convinced me that people create their own emotional reactions to events. However, it was not until the winter of 1987 that I truly understood this principle in a deeply personal way.
>
> That winter was a magical time for me. It presented the possibility of fulfilling one of my most heartfelt lifelong dreams—to trek to Mt. Everest. After meeting in New Delhi, my friend Dr. Stan Kuczaj and I headed for Kathmandu, Nepal. Our trip to the Khumbu region near Mt. Everest would involve a plane ride to the village of Lukla, a landing on a tiny dirt runway on the edge of a 5,000 foot precipice, and a 14-day hike to Everest. . . . Valley walls of 5,000-15,000 feet are common, making flying in small planes a very hazardous activity.

The plane to Lukla departed only once in the morning and only in perfect weather, and for three days we spent our mornings waiting anxiously for the weather to clear. By the fourth day we began to wonder if our trip would be possible. On the fourth morning it rained and we decided to . . . take the bus to Jeri, a city near the Khumbu region, and from there hike to Everest.

We rushed to the bus station. Hordes of oxen, cattle, chickens, bike, rickshaws, and an occasional camel blocked our path. I was beginning to feel desperate. If we missed the bus our last chance to see Everest would be one plane tomorrow morning, and the weather report was bleak.

We missed the bus to Jeri by several minutes. Sitting down on the curb I felt as depressed as I can remember. A lifelong dream is a lot to lose. To come all the way to Nepal and be denied our goal—it seemed so unfair. I spent the night staring at the ceiling and listening to the rain on the roof. The next morning the weather miraculously cleared and we flew off to the mountains. What a glorious trek!

After two weeks of the most beautiful scenery I have ever experienced, we learned . . . . . the bus to Jeri had gone over a 1,000 foot cliff and all the passengers had been killed. It was clear from the date that it was OUR bus to Jeri that was doomed.

I will never forget that moment. Every detail of sight, sound, and feeling is as vivid as the day she spoke. My mind raced back to the wild cab ride to catch the bus to Jeri. Every camel, every cow, every bike in our path had instantly been transformed from my worst enemy to my best friend. . . . Without the wisdom of hindsight, we cannot know whether events are truly victories or defeats. The next time you are sure that something "terrible" has happened to you, ask yourself, "Is this the bus to Jeri?"

Self-Efficacy/Self-Confidence

Self-efficacy is essentially self-confidence within a specific context. The concept of self-confidence is often over-generalized as a trait you have from birth, as if you were somehow given the ability to meet every challenge with all the right stuff to be successful. It is ridiculous to think, however, that anybody is confident in everything they do. By contrast, almost everyone has a degree of self-confidence in something.

When you are experiencing flow, you have a greater sense of self-efficacy. In that moment you feel confident that you can execute whatever task you're determined to do, and that you can do so over and over again. Self-efficacy is an acquired state—one that comes with extensive experience. The more self-confidence you can muster, the greater the chance you'll have a successful outcome. Self-confidence takes time to develop, and it's dependent upon you to make it grow.

Understand that self-efficacy is not a skill or competency all by itself. Instead it emerges through the use of strategy and experience. If we take a moment and review some of the previous strategies mentioned here, you will see the word *confidence* used by individuals who were employing other strategies to find their flow. Consider:

A female college student (AM) describing the use of visualization and preparation to help build confidence:

> With test-taking I do some visualization but more preparation. When I prepare for a test I think about doing it, I think about answering questions, and it gives me confidence.

As already mentioned, building self-efficacy is a matter of building on previous success. A female college student (KM) recognizes that once flow occurs, by its very presence it builds confidence, among other benefits:

> I would like to get into as many flow experiences as possible. Things feel up and up when you are in that state. I'm more confident, more positive, more willing to help others, and more happy.

In interview after interview, topic after topic, individuals who discovered flow did so in and through their ability to tap into their own sense of self-confidence, whether they used strategies of visualization, positive self-talk, organizing themselves, remembering past memories of success, or simply being in a place where they felt most comfortable. That ability to believe in oneself and one's abilities to do the job in the moment is a valuable asset and a constant companion for the high-performing individual.

Emotional Strategies

Emotions are powerful. They rule and reign over everything we do. In any circumstance they can either enhance or destroy what we're experiencing. Feelings such as joy, happiness, contentment, and enjoyment place us firmly in the moment, while emotions such as fear, self-doubt, anger, or resentment can pull us out of our current experience.

A prevalent topic in leadership today is Emotional Intelligence (EQ). Stated simply, EQ is the process of recognizing and understanding your own emotions as well as the ability to recognize and understand the emotions of others. The purpose: translating feelings into understanding.

EQ has been found to be highly learnable, in contrast to IQ which is more fixed. Those with a high EQ find themselves performing better and with greater job success than those individuals with only high IQs.[41]

We've all seen this—the brilliant kid who couldn't get the job or make it in the real world. Then there's our buddy down the street who used to skip school, barely made it through math class and is now running his or her own successful business. The difference often lies in people's ability to understand and manage the emotions of themselves and of others.

Flow entry is easier when you're in a positive mood or when you're feeling appreciative or grateful or happy. Consider for a moment AR, a female college student, who describes how she feels when she runs:

> I was going jogging in the morning. As I was ending the jog, I went about 2 ½ miles and felt like I could keep going. I was really enjoying the activity. It was kind of like a "runner's high" in a way. I felt complete concentration in what I was doing and a feeling of happiness.

Others experienced in finding flow have described themselves as successfully regulating their emotions in ways such as activating positive emotions, removing negative emotions, or tapping into such emotions as enthusiasm and playfulness.

One female college student (HK) defended the importance of using self-talk to not only generate positive thoughts and feelings, but also to disregard or filter out negative feelings: "I validate myself and say how I am worth it. I do not think you can have flow and feel like piece of crap. You have to feel good about yourself."

Emotions are usually the result of either external or internal experiences that must be interpreted by the brain. Therefore the gateway to emotion is through our conscious thinking. This takes us back to strategies of mental rehearsal and self-talk, both of which are the gatekeepers of emotion.

Physical Strategies

Calming Down

Physical strategies related to flow entry are mainly about your ability to manage arousal, including your personal energy level. (Other physical strategies will be discussed briefly within the Personal Management category in the next chapter.)

For most of us some degree of stress is a constant companion. Hans Selye, the famous psychologist, called this Eustress or good stress,[42] and it is an essential component of stretching ourselves to achieve. However, individuals achieving flow often find that they were relaxed and physically calm, not uptight. From deep breathing exercises to taking a bath, from meditation to yoga—such tools help would-be flow finders control their bodies and manage the level of their arousal to keep themselves under control despite their circumstances. We have all experienced anxiety or depression and every mental and physical state in-between, yet most of us lack the skills to manage such states very well. In addition, every MLA we engage in may require a different level of energy based on its challenge or circumstance. How the football player and the surgeon prepare to begin their performances is obviously quite different.

One male college student (DR) discusses the value of calming himself to usher in the flow experience:

> Calmness readies you. You have to be calm because it allows you not to be caught up in one single emotion or frustration in your mind or whatever it is that is happening, that you can kind of pull away, you can regroup all your energies and resources, you kind of get everything ready and primed. A tiger that is calm, it gets stiller and crouches and gets ready to pounce right before the attack. Somehow that's what calmness does, the grouping, the freeing of your mind, everything is ready to perform better.

70

Meditation is mentioned by many people as a core strategy for calming down or setting the stage for flow. Meditation relaxes and decreases levels of arousal, often prompting higher levels of focus and personal control.[43] [44] [45] It's clear that relaxation methods and strategies of meditation often transcend the mere physical and prompt a spiritual experience that can lead to a state of flow.

Others speak of how meditating impacts their entire day. A male attorney says, "On days when I have meditated, my whole day seems to go with a kind of flow." This is consistent with the assertion that many of the techniques of meditation or spiritual disciplines can assist individuals over time in their natural balancing of both challenges and skills.[46]

Psyching Up

In contrast to strategies that are designed to relax and calm down the mind and body, other tactics help raise—appropriately—the level of arousal and personal energy. Such is the case with young football players who, before a big game, pump each other up with rituals such as butting heads, smacking each other around, listening to inspiring or loud music, and generally moving into a higher level of physical energy. As one high school senior asserted, "To start it, a lot of the time it is listening to a song, a little bit more on the hard side. It just kind of gets me going, gets me thinking of the game." MB, also a high school senior, spoke of another interesting strategy for generating high energy: "I always put my helmet on, and there is this one kid on the team, and I hit him three times. We always head butt each other three times, and that really gets the energy and adrenaline going."

A female high school student (AH) made a similar comment: "Sometimes I play a little fast music to get me pumped up, not to the point where I am nervous but just excited and ready to go."

This is in stark contrast to the brain surgeon preparing to perform a procedure that may require delicate movements in a physical area no larger than a centimeter. Is getting pumped up to loud music the right pre-performance strategy? Of course not. The surgeon will most likely be playing baroque or other types of classical or soothing music, taking deep breaths and visualizing the procedure, all to ready his or her fingers for the micro movements that are soon to be needed.

Though you may be neither a football player nor a brain surgeon, you can probably attest to the value of having the right energy level for the arena you are playing in. Whether you're preparing to give a presentation and are overly anxious, or you're working on a dull project and need a boost, seeking out your best arousal and energy level could help you enter a flow state.

CHAPTER 6: Time-Based Strategies

While all the external and internal strategies discussed thus far may be considered self-regulation strategies, several strategies can be categorized by time. More specifically, the use of such tools depends on how far away you are from actually being in the zone.

Effort Regulation Strategies

Whether you're just entering or already in a flow state, a choice of several strategies may help you sustain this experience. These may include the following: giving yourself permission to enter flow, just doing it, applying consistent effort, tapping into determination, giving full effort, finding a rhythm, being persistent, pushing yourself to stay engaged, using breaks or time-outs when appropriate, and staying the course until a particular goal is achieved. Taken together, these are methods used to keep progress going and to manage the experience while it is taking place. While many people in the midst of flow claim that they are not actually *thinking* and may be more or less oblivious, some admit they do use such strategies, or perhaps they do so by subconscious habit.

Is determination a strategy? Perhaps. As such, think of it as your ability to tap into a deep sense of purpose, energy, and will. Similar to self-confidence, determination enables you to find and make use of other strategies. As EP, a doctor, explains, "I am trying my hardest, I am putting forth all of my effort. I pray, I ponder, I study, I do all I can."

Preparation Strategies—Just Before Flow

Preparation of some sort is crucial for entering a flow state. In planning ahead for a productive period of activity, we might ask,

"What do I need to do to have everything ready so flow can occur?" Answers to this question include such organizing behaviors as making lists, gathering your tools and resources, compartmentalizing tools and tasks, pre-thinking strategies, prioritizing and scheduling actions, studying and processing the upcoming event, contingency planning, initiating rituals and habits, making sure that there will be variety in the experience, and warming up your body and mind to slip into the moment.

Similar to the way athletes value warming up for a big competition, others may warm up to wake up the body more fully, get a project or assignment started, begin a complex drawing, or enter into a particular character prior to acting on stage.

BC, a professional educator, tells of his preparation strategies for a writing project and how challenging it can be to focus his energies:

> For my writing, flow does not come immediately. In fact, there is an ongoing joke that I have a prerequisite of two or two and a half hours of sitting and staring at the screen. It just does not come, so only after I have paid my dues, I allow myself to eliminate other thoughts and concentrate on the task at hand. I am a bit of a binge writer. It takes so long to get into it that I am riding that wave until I am completely out.

Preparation may require being comfortable in ways such as prepping a particular space, wearing comfortable clothes, and finding a comfortable position so as to limit distractions. One woman describes first making herself comfortable by finding the right position on the couch or on the bed, and by getting enough pillows and blankets. "I kind of work from the inside out," she comments.

Rituals or routines are used by many who would loosen up to enter flow. Common among athletes, surgeons, and other performers, the use of rituals provides a base of consistency that allows a particular set of behaviors to come forth, often helping the individual "to divert attention away from negative, irrelevant information."[47] As a male college senior (RB) comments, "When I was going to play college ball, I would try to do the same activities and they would be nurturing to me. Doing the exact same things on game day would soothe me." And feeling soothed aids his flow.

Middle-aged professionals and older, more experienced participants in my workshops also speak of their routines and rituals. A male doctor said:

> I usually get so completely absorbed in work, time
> flies by and I do not even give it much thought. I
> attribute this to a routine and familiarity with what
> I am doing.

Creating art also inspires routines. Writers, for example, are known for their unique rituals which help them slip into flow. One novelist, for example, developed a routine of writing during long daily train commutes, so that his psyche became accustomed to the sound and movement and he would enter a flow state as soon as he boarded the train. Another clears his desk of all but his computer, note cards, and a single pen, and plays wordless music very loud until everything else is blocked out of his mind but his current creative project. Still another describes how she takes a second cup of coffee and closes the door to her office, then looks up at her bulletin board which contains photos and quotes that help propel her into the zone.[48]
In all the ritualized strategies people mention, what they're seeking is a type of consistency, a constant and repeating group of behaviors to assist them in generating flow.

Scheduling your time, finding the right time and place to let go into flow, is another preparation strategy. An experienced male doctor mentions the value of having a scheduled day to allow him to focus on one patient at a time: "A schedule is really helpful and routine. I plan the day, at least in my mind, where I am going to go."

An attorney found routine helpful in balancing his family and work life, including periods conducive to flow activities. "It's knowing that certain things have to happen at a certain period of the day." Comments like these are consistent with time management literature that suggests there are optimal times to schedule internal activities, external activities, and self-focused activities.[49]

Another professional talks of setting the stage to open himself up to flow: "When I identify those things which I can choose to do, I set the stage which puts me in harmony with other people, with myself, with God, and all is right there, which is a choice that I make, that opens me up to flow."

Scheduling yourself, then, is an active process that helps clarify values, set priorities, and focus energies—each vital to finding your flow.

Personal Management Strategies

Indirect strategies also provide a foundation for flow to take place, including maintaining your physical health through proper exercise and eating habits. Hinting of Maslow's hierarchy of needs,[50] it can be hypothesized that you may have more difficulty with higher-order functioning, even self-actualization or flow, if you don't have the proper foundation of physical fitness, health and wellness.[51]

A former tennis player turned attorney (RJ) still experiences flow on the tennis court:

> How do you get into flow? It is working out and getting into great shape, then getting the techniques right, then perfecting those techniques.

Hopefully it culminates in flow, when you are playing that most important match, where all of it wells up, the past and the preparation for that wells up right in that one moment and it clicks.

Exercise provides not only an opportunity for physical release, but also the arousal needed to maintain alertness. Two doctors, one mid-career and one at the end of his career, mention that exercise provides them with a higher level of alertness or a rush of adrenaline, thus offering the energy they need to find flow. For a professional mediating attorney, exercise is a place for receiving inspiration and for knowing how to deal with difficult challenges. "When I was exercising today," she reports, "it just came in my mind how to set up my coaching session and how I'd do my intervention with him [a young boy]. It just fell right into place."

Another personal management strategy is sufficient rest and recovery time. This includes not only getting ample sleep each night (6-8 hours), but also taking mini-breaks throughout the day (approximately every hour) in order to restore lost energy. One female college student (SH) comments, "I mentioned earlier that fatigue is a distraction. I have to be getting proper rest." Such comments, often mentioned along with proper nutrition and other personal management issues, highlight the value of taking care of one's body so that important mental activities are not disrupted by poor health.

There is also value in living a balanced life and doing the little things that make you feel safe and content. Such strategies may include getting a weekly massage, spending time with friends, taking walks in the woods, going shopping or to a movie, writing in a journal, or engaging in a hobby or any one of a number of self-improvement activities. Whatever your personal inclinations, such activities ground you and help you ready yourself for flow.

Taken together the major themes for Finding Your Flow can be summarized in the following illustration:

Choosing the Right Environment

Placing oneself in an environment that is conductive to generating a flow experience (i.e., a dance hall, operating room, office the mountains etc...t.

Environment Regulation

Regulating the environment to enhance or support a flow experience (i.e., changing temperature, lighting, furniture arrange-ment, etc...).

Interpersonal Regulation

Managing life relationships to decrease inter-personal interferences, allowing one to have greater levels of focus.

— Spiritual Strategies

Strategies of the spirit - primarily to engage higher forces (i.e., prayer, humility, deeper purposes of self, etc...)

— Philosophical Strategies

Strategies of philosophy (i.e., beliefs, principles, attitudes, perspectives, rules, standards. etc...).

— Psychological Strategies

Strategies of the mind (i.e., goals, self-talk, focus, visualization, etc...)

— Emotional Strategies

Strategies of the heart - primarily generating the right affect or mood.

— Physical Strategies

Strategies of the body - primarily for raising or lowering arousal.

Self Regulation Strategies

Effort Regulation

Choosing when and how to enter flow, managing personal state during flow

Preparation

General preparation, practice and administration. prior to the flow experience.

Personal Management

General life management strategies (i.e., ample sleep, nutrition, massages, and other general health concerns etc..., in order to build a base-line of wellness.

CHAPTER 7: It's All About Focus

Every flow strategy we've been discussing is either a flow asset or a liability, contributing to or hindering flow. If a particular flow strategy is neutral, it is irrelevant and can be ignored.

In reviewing all the factors just discussed, you'll recognize that each one has its own time and place. Developing an awareness of their time and place will solidify how all the factors/strategies fit together to contribute to present moment focus—the essence of flow. By becoming more aware of where you are placing your attention, you can tell if you are actually in the moment or somewhere else (outside vs. inside; future vs. past, etc.), processing and preparing for flow.

Flow Focus and Strategies Map

Now let's illustrate the idea of developing "flexible focus" by mapping out and clustering all of the factors/strategies (which are either Flow Assets or Flow Liabilities) using a nine-quadrant model. This model helps you understand where you are placing your focus and using your energies, and how each quadrant is necessary to support present moment focus and flow.

We can break down this model of focus by first identifying whether we are focusing inside or outside of ourselves, then how broadly or narrowly we are placing our focus.

Let's clarify these first two dimensions by using a football quarterback as an example. To execute a play a quarterback must first review a number of possible plays in his mind (internal/broad focus or IB), then make a decision about which play will be executed (internal/narrow focus or IN).

Once at the line of scrimmage, the quarterback waits for the snap from his center (external/narrow focus or EN), then once the ball is in hand scans the field and identifies a number of players that he could throw the ball to (external/broad focus or EB). Once he finds his man, he executes his pass (external/narrow focus or EN) and completes the play. Notice that each step of the play requires a different type of focus for the play (the moment of performance) to be successful[52] and that each type of focus is necessary to execute the actual play.

Daily challenges, while taking place in a different arena and often not as compressed in time, often follow the same pattern as that of our quarterback.

Let's begin at the top of the model. We read our External Broad environment (EB) to assess situations. We look through a group of people in a meeting before finding someone we need to talk to. We look at industry data or macro-economic data to understand the context of our issues. This is the forest—it's the big picture. With this big picture information we are then better able to look at the specifics that are right in front of us—our immediate space, such as being in conversation, writing an email or cleaning our desk. This an External Narrow focus or (EN).

At the bottom of the model you see the Internal Broad Self (IB) and the Internal Narrow self (IN). We look broadly when we are assessing our thoughts, feelings, physical states, or when generally scanning to address our overall internal states of being. We often use this type of focus to visualize ideas or options and to be creative. We step into the Internal Narrow self when we isolate specific thoughts, feelings, or issues that require decisions to be made and actions to be taken. Notice that in both the External Broad self (IB) or the Internal Narrow self (IN) we are tapping into areas that include the spiritual, philosophical, psychological, emotional or physical parts of self.

These first four vertical quadrants help us understand that a successful flowing performance requires several different types of focus working together, though each serves a different function or system.

Looking at the horizontal quadrants to this model, we might add the dimension of time. On the left side of the model you have your LP or Long Past and your SP or Short Past. Individuals who look far back, who reminisce, analyze their history, ponder long and forgotten memories hang out in this place. This was the intent of Freudian psychoanalysis and other types of psychotherapies that focus on deep and extended client histories in order to help root out deep conflicts, thus releasing clients from the burdens of their past.

These types of focus tap into a person's history to help clarify the development of personal values, self-confidence, individual philosophy, and the development of personal wisdom—even how one ascribes meaning to personal experiences. By contrast, individuals looking at the short past are reflecting on a performance moment, assessing themselves against a standard or learning from a recently completed experience. Athletes, pilots, military personnel, and highly motivated workers or performers often review their most recent performances to gather feedback, assess their effectiveness, and learn from each and every experience.

The quadrant LF represents Long Future. It is here that one pays attention to things like missions and life visions, a way to look strategically at long-term planning. Clarifying one's mission and detailing one's vision, setting long-term goals, etc., are strategies that set the stage for present moment focus and flow. SF represents Short Future. Here we are looking to plan ahead, but only on a short-term basis. It is here where we may set daily, weekly, or monthly goals. Such stage-setting and structure prepares us for being in the moment because the future is neither clear nor set.

We can add the concept of duration: how long we keep our attention in any one place. Putting all of these quadrants together gives us an opportunity to increase our awareness and to recognize where our attention is and how it supports our present moment focus. This Flow Focus and Strategies Map allows us to map out all of the potential factors (defined as either Flow Assets or Flow Liabilities) that either contribute to or detract from our flow.

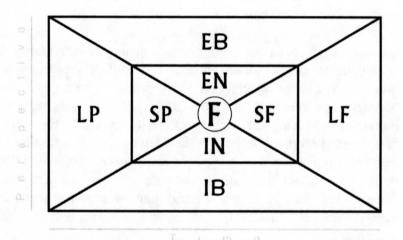

Notice in the second model, the IN and IB quadrants have been replaced with you, the central figure, who controls all of the internal systems and processes necessary to lead you towards and through all of your moments of performance.

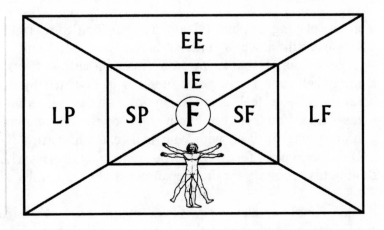

At the very center of the pictured map is where our attention is fixed and where we are completely in the moment. We are not thinking about the future or the past. We are not thinking outside ourselves or inside ourselves. Neither are we thinking broadly or narrowly. Everything we experience is completely focused on the here and now without interruption. We are present, absorbed in the now—here.

While all we really have is each moment, you can see from this model that how we place our attention each moment is often somewhere other than in the "now". Think about this for a moment: you are at lunch with a friend only to be thinking about an issue at work that needs to be solved this afternoon (short-future focus—SF) or in six months (long-future focus—LF). Or you are driving home from a date and thinking about how it went (short-past focus—SP). You process this experience by comparing it to other dates further back (long-past focus—LP). Pondering either situation keeps you from paying attention to the most important aspect of the moment—the road!

You are playing a round of golf and you don't feel right. You assess what the issue is (internal-broad focus—IB) only to find that your back is bothering you (internal-narrow focus—IN). During that same round your attention is thwarted by a slight breeze that you feel is affecting your swing (external-broad focus—EB). You then re-set your sights on the flag and hole that you are trying to reach with your ball (external-narrow focus—EN). Either type of focus keeps you from being present with each shot, but is necessary for the preparation and set-up of that shot.

In this simple model every factor connected to flow can be sorted, placed, and better understood as to whether it supports or hinders the flow experience. Learning to recognize these quadrants enhances your awareness about where your attention is at any given moment and where you wish it to be. Taken collectively, being in the zone is about being focused in the moment itself (the very middle of the model—like a target or bull's-eye).

Flow can be woven into everyday life by raising the probability of its presence. But how does one do this? Is there a particular formula that we can all use to get into the zone? Is there a step-by-step process we can all rely on to make our performance better? I believe there is, and it's simpler than you think.

Certainly, we are each unique. Your fingerprints, voice, iris, physique, personality, gait, energy and thousands of other factors are your very own. How we experience what we do is absolutely unique to each of us as well. While we find ourselves with the basic building blocks of life, we alone must choose how to cultivate our potential.

Remember the story about the man who boasted to the local vicar after transforming his property from a jungle to a beautiful garden? "Don't forget," admonished the cleric, "God had some part to play in the process." "Well," said the man, "you should have seen it when God had it all to himself." A nice way to remind ourselves that wherever the building blocks of life come from, how we use and arrange them is up to each of us.

Consider another example. In the 1991 blockbuster hit *City Slickers*, Billy Crystal, Daniel Stern, and Bruno Kirby portrayed three mid-career professionals as they struggled to get out of their corporate skin and assume more adventurous selves. Their leader was a rather intimidating cowboy named Curley who led the group on a real out-West cattle drive. Throughout their tumultuous adventure, this group of city slickers noticed something special about Curley. It was his philosophy of life. Somehow they came to believe that this sometimes crude man had the answers they were all looking for.

During one of their deep discussions about the purpose and meaning of life, a rather gruff Curley explained his simple yet profound mantra that life was all about the "one thing." The character played by Billy Crystal was anxious to discover what that one thing was, but he kept getting the same response from the old Yoda-like cowboy: "It's about the one thing." In desperation, Billy kept pushing, until Curly paused for moment, looked intently at his mentee and said, "You've got to figure that out for yourself."

In that spirit, it's time for us to follow the same advice. We've begun the process by discussing some of the basic themes and the specific strategies people use to find their flow. Now let's take this awareness to the next level to help you find *your* flow.

Section III: Finding *Your* Flow

CHAPTER 8: The 720° Sweep

As we've seen, entering a flow state can depend on a multitude of factors, from how energetic you feel to how focused you are, and from how you feel to what's driving you. With so many interrelated factors needing to work in unison, when even one or two factors are out of whack, that can have a significant impact on your ability to get where you want to be.

Think of the last time you had a pebble in your shoe. Something so small, yet so annoying. Out of the countless factors and systems working in concert to facilitate walking, that one small irritant demanded the bulk of your attention.

To achieve your best, therefore, requires a process of self-awareness in which you learn to identify what your own vital flow factors are, and which one or two might be keeping you out of flow.

Now we are going to go through what I call the 720-degree sweep. It is called the 720-degree sweep because it is designed to have you do a 360-degree internal analysis as well as a 360-degree external analysis of a current flow arena. Taken together you will conduct a 720-degree sweep of the Meaningful Life Arena you wish to improve.

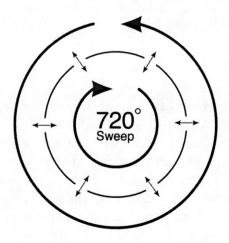

This process will broaden your awareness of the factors that make up the parts of your internal Ferrari and your external race track, including questions that tap into the past, present, and future. The questions that you are about to answer have been boiled down from more than 158 individual strategies as revealed by surveys and in-depth interviews with people from diverse backgrounds and experiences. They represent all nine quadrants in the Flow Focus and Strategies Map. When answering these questions, remember that while we are laying out many of the most prevalent concepts and strategies that people use to facilitate their flow experiences, it's not an exhaustive list. You will have an opportunity to add other factors specific to your own state of flow. Once you have rated yourself against these Flow Assets and Liabilities, we will then narrow your focus to one or two areas in order to start your first training mission.

First take a moment to decide in which arena you'd like to consider these questions. Each life arena will have its own performance formula, so that what works in one arena may not work in another. Decide whether you want to answer the questions about your work, home life, a hobby, sport, or any other arena on which you'd like to concentrate right now.

On the line below, state the Meaningful Life Arena (MLA) that you would most like to review:

Notice that each question is followed by a scale from 1-10, where 1 represents a complete lack of either awareness or skill in a particular area (essentially this is what you consider your greatest weaknesses, major hindrances, or greatest liabilities for achieving flow). In contrast, a 10 would represent a major strength or flow asset. This would be something that you already habitually do and that you feel is a major contributor to your states of flow and peak experience. Between 1 and 10 would, of course, represent various levels of strength and weakness.

Feel free to skip questions that don't relate to your situation. I suggest you take a minute or two for each question, allowing a bit extra for those that are most thought provoking. This way the entire self-analysis will take you about an hour, or at most two. You can, of course, break the exercise up into briefer segments of time if you prefer.

Step 1: Self-Analysis

The Physical Environment

1. The Place Itself. Some people find their flow by simply going to a certain place, whether out in nature or in a more structured environment, such as a surgical theater or a dance studio, or in a certain room in your house. Now consider the arena that you wish to assess and answer the following question:

How successful are you at placing yourself in a place that is conducive to your peak states of performance?

1 2 3 4 5 6 7 8 9 10

2. Setting the Stage. If the space you're in isn't already conducive to flow, you can make changes. From making adjustments to lighting, adding beautiful pictures, plants, inspirational messages, or modifying the temperature, etc., each prop helps to set the stage for flow.

How effective are you at managing your physical environment?

1 2 3 4 5 6 7 8 9 10

3. Organizing the Stage. Think about how you engineer the physical space to insure that everything is in its proper order so that you can stay focused in the moment. Note: a desk facing into the bright sun is not conducive to flow.

How well do you keep this flow arena organized and in order?

1 2 3 4 5 6 7 8 9 10

4. Minimizing Distractions. Anything from a ringing phone, to people coming in and out of a given space, or perhaps the weather itself can affect your focus. It's important to be aware of external distractions and have a set of strategies to deal with them or to insure that they don't interfere with your experience.

How effective are you at removing external distractions?

1 2 3 4 5 6 7 8 9 10

Interpersonal Regulation

5. People Enjoyment. Certain flow activities are shared with other people. In fact, research on job satisfaction suggests that up to 70 percent of your experience is impacted by your relationship with others.

If your flow arena includes others, how much do you enjoy being around the people that reside there or move in and out of it?

1 2 3 4 5 6 7 8 9 10

6. Communicating Clearly. Flow is often experienced with and through others, and your and their interpersonal skill-sets often play a role. It can be frustrating to work with someone who does not understand what you mean to say. Being in sync with your co-workers, team-mates, partners, etc., makes a big difference.

Now consider the flow arena that you are assessing, and if it includes others with whom you need to communicate effectively, rate your capacity to communicate effectively with them.

1   2   3   4   5   6   7   8   9   10

7. Listening to Others. Your ability to take information and use it for appropriate action and decision-making is important to tap into flow—especially when others are involved in the process.

Rate your capacity to listen or capture information from others effectively within this flow arena.

1   2   3   4   5   6   7   8   9   10

8. Interpersonal Conflict. Another variable is your current relationship status with the others in your flow arena. If you have hidden negative feelings, grudges, or simply don't like a person, this can be distracting and diminish your flow.

How effective are you at managing negative feelings, grudges or conflict with others that reside in this flow arena?

1   2   3   4   5   6   7   8   9   10

9. Support _for_ Others. You may find yourself in synergy with others because your relationships with them are positive and supported by your thoughts and feelings towards them.

To what degree do you actively (directly or indirectly) support, affirm or have positive relationships with others within this flow arena?

1   2   3   4   5   6   7   8   9   10

10. Support *from* Others. It is often apparent that each person plays a specific role or roles that allow you to focus on what you need to focus on to enter flow. A competent secretarial staff serves a major function for a small business, especially if they do their job well. If your flow arena under assessment includes others, then rate them (and yourself):

How well do you utilize the knowledge, skills, and abilities of others to support you in your flow arena?

1 2 3 4 5 6 7 8 9 10

11. Feedback from Others. Feedback comes from many sources, including other people. Feedback may be positive or negative, and the frequency with which it is provided matters, depending on the arena. Modern practices in organizations suggest conducting a performance review as few as one and as many as four times a year. Yet this may not be enough. There are times we need constant feedback to make adjustments to our behavior so as to stay on track and reach our goals. An airplane is rarely "on course" but always making micro adjustments throughout its journey. Human beings have the same need, especially in relationships.

How well do you obtain and implement feedback from others in this flow arena?

1 2 3 4 5 6 7 8 9 10

12. Synergy with Others. When groups or teams are in synergy, working well together, they emerge as greater than the sum of their parts (1+1+1 = 4+). By contrast, when they are not in synergy they may equal something less (1+1+1 = 2-). As you consider all of the factors contributing to or detracting from your interpersonal experiences, rate your level of synergy with others within this flow arena:

1 2 3 4 5 6 7 8 9 10

Spiritual Strategies

13. Tapping into a Higher Power. Finding your flow may not be only about you but about something that is bigger. For some, it's God, while for others a higher power. Considering your flow arena and ask yourself:

How effective are you at tapping into a power or force higher or larger than yourself?

1   2   3   4   5   6   7   8   9   10

14. Belief System. Having a core belief system is a key stabilizing and supporting factor that can contribute to your flow. Some have a more grounded and consistent belief system while others have a less developed belief system. Consider yours:

How well does your core belief system serve and support you in this flow arena?

1   2   3   4   5   6   7   8   9   10

15. On Purpose? Being on purpose taps into deep reservoirs of personal energy. Consider how well this flow arena supports and affirms your core purpose.

How "on purpose" are you within this particular flow arena?

1   2   3   4   5   6   7   8   9   10

16. Self-Belief. Research suggests that a common factor contributing to success is believing in yourself and in the world around you. Self-efficacy is the ability to be confident within a particular arena. If you believe that you have the ability to be successful, then you have developed self-efficacy for that arena. But what if the world around you doesn't seem supportive?

How well do your current beliefs about yourself and the world support your ability to find flow in this arena?

1   2   3   4   5   6   7   8   9   10

17. *Minimizing Self-Judgment*. Making errors or poor choices, or not doing as well as you'd hoped, may lead to self-deprecating attitudes. It is crucial to learn how to separate yourself from your performance, removing your ego from particular outcomes. Doing this frees you to go through new experiences without fear and instead focus on the here and now.

How effective are you at letting go of personal judgment and/or forgiving yourself for past mistakes within this flow arena?

1   2   3   4   5   6   7   8   9   10

18. *Comparing Self to Others*. When competing, comparing your own performance with that of others may come naturally but may cause feelings of frustration or self-loathing. While we often look for benchmarks to compare our performance to, this keeps us from paying attention to our own strengths and weaknesses and attending fully to our own experience. Comparing yourself to others is a trap that rarely adds value.

How able are you to refrain from comparing yourself to others and/or appreciate your own strengths and weaknesses within this flow arena?

1   2   3   4   5   6   7   8   9   10

19. *Core Values Connection*. Finding your flow depends on focusing your energy in a certain direction based on your core values. This direction must be significant if you are to engage fully in the process.

To what degree are your core values being served within this particular flow arena?

1   2   3   4   5   6   7   8   9   10

20. Letting Go of the Outcome. If you feel scared or intimidated by an expected outcome in a given arena, then that fear will be at the top of your mind. Someone may have asked you NOT to think of a pink elephant, only to prove the point that trying NOT to pay attention prompts you to pay attention to that thing even harder. The way to produce an effective outcome is to focus solely on the process.

How well are you able to let go of thoughts of outcomes in order to enter flow?

$$1 \quad 2 \quad 3 \quad 4 \quad 5 \quad 6 \quad 7 \quad 8 \quad 9 \quad 10$$

Philosophical Strategies

21. Having a Personal Philosophy. Deep down each one of us has a philosophy, often developed over years of experience and through a personal process of cultivating and applying important ideas. Personal philosophies can include such things as beliefs, principles ideas, attitudes, perspectives, qualities, virtues, and personal standards.

Do you have a guiding philosophy that drives your behaviors within this flow arena?

$$1 \quad 2 \quad 3 \quad 4 \quad 5 \quad 6 \quad 7 \quad 8 \quad 9 \quad 10$$

22. Applying your Personal Philosophy. How well do you make use of your philosophy within your flow arena?

Do you have certain ideas, phrases, or principles that you keep at the top of your mind that help you stay focused in this arena?

$$1 \quad 2 \quad 3 \quad 4 \quad 5 \quad 6 \quad 7 \quad 8 \quad 9 \quad 10$$

Psychological Strategies

23. Setting Goals. Goal-setting is an essential building block of flow, and we'll have a full section on how to set them intelligently a bit later. Meanwhile, the research is clear: People who intentionally set goals outperform those who do not. Setting goals channels your energy and, designed properly, such goals provide precise feedback about which objectives are being met.

How well do you set challenging yet achievable goals that focus your thoughts and actions within this flow arena?

1   2   3   4   5   6   7   8   9   10

24. Intrinsic Motivation. Finding your flow is often associated with enjoyment of an activity for its own sake and without concern for external reward.

How intrinsically motivated are you in your chosen flow arena? Are you interested because of external rewards or because of a love for what you do?

1   2   3   4   5   6   7   8   9   10

25. Positive Self-Talk. The average human being can produce as many as 53,000 thoughts a day. Your internal dialogue is like a thermostat, affecting the level of your emotions: "That's the third time Gwen has taken credit for my work. This needs to stop," or "What a beautiful day. I love the beauty of the mountains." At issue is our ability to recognize and control this jet stream of internal language and dialogue, rather than being its slave, letting circumstances dictate how we feel.

How effective are you in managing negative self-talk and generating positive thoughts, images or attitudes within this flow arena?

1   2   3   4   5   6   7   8   9   10

26. Multiple Perspectives. Have you ever had an issue that made you feel completely stuck, where you could only see the problem from a single fixed point? Compare this to a time where you were able to sort through a problem or issue by looking at it from several vantage points. Perhaps a friend, family member, or colleague talked you through a different way of looking at some event, maybe using a more long-term perspective, a more humorous perspective, a more practical perspective, or any perspective that helped you move beyond your stuck-ness.

Rate your ability to access different perspectives and/or see situations more clearly within this flow arena:

1   2   3   4   5   6   7   8   9   10

27. Broad Focus. When we speak about flow, we talk a lot about the principle of focus or paying attention to the most vital aspects of our experience. We don't spend as much time discussing broad focus. You have heard the phrase "Can't see the forest for the trees," meaning that when you are overly focused on the details it is difficult to see the whole picture. While hitting a forehand over the net and into the back corner takes focused attention in the narrow sense, you must step back and be aware of what is coming back to you so that you can prepare for the next shot. In a similar vein, it is difficult for anyone to make an important decision without considering the impact of the decision in the long-term. Now consider your current flow arena and rate your level of broad awareness.

How effective are your skills of awareness? Can you see broadly to better understand the context?

1   2   3   4   5   6   7   8   9   10

28. Narrow Focus. Thoughts, feelings, negative attitudes, other people, the weather—just about anything inside or outside you can compete for your attention. You are constantly engaging with the world and much data is being thrown at you. Some of it is relevant and other parts are completely irrelevant. For instance, you're driving your car in a snowstorm with your family in the back seat. Your tires slip on some ice and are starting to spin.

Everyone is screaming and the outside elements are putting you in a difficult situation. Do you pay attention to the weather, the sounds of the voices in the backseat, or do you focus on adjusting the wheel and seeking to control the spin?

How well do you filter out irrelevant thoughts, feelings, attitudes, or negative external stimuli so as to focus only on what is most important?

1   2   3   4   5   6   7   8   9   10

29. Now Focused. Regardless of what quadrant you are (e.g., external vs. internal, broad vs. narrow, past vs. present vs. future, etc.) you are paying attention to something, then shifting that attention to something else. The question is, how long can you sustain your focus? Sometimes we are focused in the future, and then turn to the past. Sometimes we are focused on our external environment, then shift to our thoughts and feelings inside. However, when engaged in the moment of an activity your focus needs to be in the present and stay in the present without a wandering mind.

Please rate your current capacity to keep a present moment focus for extended periods of time within this flow arena.

1   2   3   4   5   6   7   8   9   10

30. Knowledge Level. No matter how many techniques you learn to increase your flow, nothing compensates for a lack of knowledge and skill in what you are doing. Finding your flow as a complete beginner in any area is rare, unless the activity provides only a moderate degree of challenge for you. Take, for instance, sweeping a floor while listening to music. You may have little experience with the process but learn it within a few seconds. Once mastered, you can turn on your iPod and sweep away, losing yourself in time and space until the job is done. In your current flow arena:

Rate your current knowledge, skills, and abilities within this flow arena.

1   2   3   4   5   6   7   8   9   10

31. Visualization. The capacity to see in your mind's eye is one of the most vital skill-sets of anyone who seeks flow and high performance. Can you see yourself "in" the moment before it happens?

How clearly can you picture in advance what you wish to accomplish within this flow arena?

1   2   3   4   5   6   7   8   9   10

32. Memories of Success/Self-Confidence Building. Can you remember a time when you performed at your best and experienced flow? Do you remember what this looked like, felt like, sounded like? When you reflect on such times, does your self-confidence increase? Perhaps you have a deep reservoir of experiences that you draw from that improves your self-confidence. Or perhaps this well is shallow and you have not build up a visual library of best performances.

How effective are you in remembering and re-generating your self-confidence by identifying past memories of success within this flow arena?

1   2   3   4   5   6   7   8   9   10

Emotional Strategies

33. Labeling Emotion. Emotions play a powerful role in our experiences and offer us insights and affect decision-making. Yet most of us fail to read our emotions with accuracy and therefore make decisions based on information we can hardly understand. If you are keenly aware of your emotions, you can use them to help you navigate your current challenges. If your emotions get the best of you, they may be a liability. However, if your emotions serve you and you are good at understanding and controlling them, then perhaps you see them as an asset.

How effective are you at labeling your emotions and managing your feelings within this flow arena?

1   2   3   4   5   6   7   8   9   10

34. Positive Attitude. Labeling emotions is one skill-set, and learning to generate emotions is yet another. Take a moment and ponder a time when you were exceedingly happy. Now think of a time where you were highly content. What about passionate, inspired, grateful, or satisfied? Do you remember a time where you actually produced the emotions that ushered in a flow experience? Now consider your flow arena under review:

How effective are you in generating positive or happy moods within this flow arena?

1   2   3   4   5   6   7   8   9   10

35. Sense of Humor. Having a sense of humor is a real help in tempering your emotional climate when you're facing significant challenges. The famous adventure team of Eric Weihenmayer and Jeff Evans call their strategy "positive pessimism." Comments they've made include: "I'm exhausted but at least we've run out of food," or "There's a hole in my shoes, but at least my socks are wet." Such language is used to mock reality and build perspective, giving the climbers the freedom to choose their response to their situation.

How well do you use humor to manage stressful situations in this flow arena?

1   2   3   4   5   6   7   8   9   10

Physical Strategies

36. *Managing Stress*. We all get wound up from time to time, and how we deal with that affects the likelihood of finding flow. Alcohol is a stress antidote for some, but it's not much help for your focus. For others, perhaps an anti-anxiety pill is beneficial. Still others use internal strategies to manage stress. They work out, go for a walk, temper their internal voice, or sit in meditation.

How effective are you at managing stress and your physical state generally?

1   2   3   4   5   6   7   8   9   10

37. *Calming the Body*. Let's take this issue of stress to the next level and identify how long it takes you to calm yourself on demand, using whatever methods you choose. Can you do it in a few minutes or even less? Note that the great yogis and monks of the Middle and Far East developed strategies to change their body's reaction to a variety of stressful situations, from lowering their body temperature to minimizing their heart rate. Some individuals have developed a keen sense of physical self-control that testifies to the powerful mind/body connection. These skills are common among high performers who recognize that exceptional physical control means high levels of mental and emotional control. Now consider your own flow arena:

How effectively and quickly can you relax on demand?

1   2   3   4   5   6   7   8   9   10

38. *Psyching Up the Body*. Now let's assess the strategies you use to pump yourself up and generate high energy, along the lines of a battle cry used by soldiers before entering combat. Among the many strategies available are music, physical movement, inspiring messages, tapping into positive emotions. Rate yourself on your ability to increase your personal energy in order to find that perfect zone or flow:

How able are you to generate high energy when you need it?

1   2   3   4   5   6   7   8   9   10

Preparation Strategies

39. Tools and Resources. Think about your flow arena and identify what tools and resources you will need to find your flow. Are you a tennis player without a racket, an executive assistant without a phone, a sculptor without clay?

Do you have all the tools and resources you need to succeed within this flow arena?

1   2   3   4   5   6   7   8   9   10

40. Organizing your Resources. Your tools and resources must be in the right place and in proper working order. When I went with a team to Mt. Kilimanjaro a few years ago, our planning included a complete staging process of gear, food, and emergency equipment. Hundreds of hours were spent by team members in making lists, checking functionality, and having access to gear in order to ensure each day would run smoothly and without distraction. Whether you are setting up a board game or organizing your desk, having your stuff in order provides peace of mind for entering flow.

How effective are you at planning, prioritizing and allocating your physical resources prior to entering this flow arena?

1   2   3   4   5   6   7   8   9   10

41. Time Management. How you use the most precious of resources—time—dictates either success or failure. Wasting time produces poorer results, while maximizing your use of time and properly prioritizing your actions allows you a smooth transition into your moments of flow. For all activities, time must be allocated and sequenced.

How effective are you at planning, allocating and/or managing your time in preparation for this flow activity?

1   2   3   4   5   6   7   8   9   10

42. Personal Comfort. If one aspect of your physical world is off, even if your clothing is too tight, your attention will be diverted. Important also are the perfect temperature and the perfect chair or sofa on which to spend time. Consider the factors that make you comfortable and answer:

Are you able to get physically comfortable within this flow arena?

1   2   3   4   5   6   7   8   9   10

43. Contingency Planning. Sometimes the unexpected occurs to throw you off, such as when you have a perfectly planned speech, only to discover a heckler in the room. You may have organized the perfect road trip with your family only to have car trouble halfway there. Despite our efforts to plan for flow, the unexpected comes up. Are you ready for that with a plan A, even a plan B?

Do you have a contingency plan(s) in readiness for your flow experience?

1   2   3   4   5   6   7   8   9   10

44. Rituals & Routines? When great performers prepare for a peak experience, they often use certain strategies to slip into the experience. I'm sure you have heard of athletes who swear by what seem to be quirky rituals, such as wearing the same color of socks, eating the same meal, or performing the same physical pre-flow action. Baseball player Wade Boggs, before each game, would only eat poultry. During his infield practice he would take exactly 150 ground balls and would enter the batting cage at precisely 5:17 p.m. When on defense and between pitches, he would swipe the dirt in front of him with his left foot, tap his glove, and adjust his cap.[53] As you consider the flow arena in question:

Have you constructed sufficient habits and/or rituals for yourself that prompt a state of high performance?

1   2   3   4   5   6   7   8   9   10

Self-Regulation Strategies

45. Managing Flow. Flow can last for just a few seconds or several hours, partly depending on your ability to regulate contributing factors. Beyond merely controlling your focus, extended flow requires a heightened sense of awareness of what is happening in the moment and making mini-adjustments if something is out of place. As you consider your flow arena, ask yourself how quickly you become aware of issues that arise which seek to pull you out of your flow, and how well you adjust to these issues in order to slip back into it.

How effective are you at staying "in the moment" or "in the zone" of your performance once you are in it?

1   2   3   4   5   6   7   8   9   10

46. Managing Challenges. Perhaps you've undertaken a project beyond your skill-set, or you don't have enough time to do it properly. When you are confronted with overwhelm, do you let anxiety get the best of you? Do you self-destruct? Or perhaps you're able to make adjustments to the challenges. How do you eat an 800-pound elephant? That's right, one bite at a time. Lao Tsu was quoted as saying: "A journey of a thousand miles begins with a single step." Now as you consider your particular flow arena, when things get dicey as they often do, how well can you adapt:

If a challenge is too high, how effective are you in breaking down large or complex tasks into smaller or simpler ones?

1   2   3   4   5   6   7   8   9   10

47. *Creating Challenges*. Have you ever engaged in an activity that started to get boring, until you changed the nature of that task to make it more interesting? Most likely you created a challenge for yourself. I recently sought the assistance of my two boys to clear the yard of unwanted weeds, but instead of our usual routine, I not only told them that they would earn two cents per weed, but I asked them how many intact weeds pulled out with the roots they could get in 30 minutes. Rather than being a chore, it was now a competition. Both boys rushed to gather as many weeds as they could, not only to earn some money, but to show their skills as professional weed pullers.

My close friend Brad explains his process for creating challenge and interest for himself prior to teaching a university class. Instead of being completely prepared, he leaves some degree of uncertainty in his presentation, forcing him to be more spontaneous and challenged as he actually engages his students.

If a challenge is too low, how effective are you in making the task more challenging or more complex to increase your engagement?

1 2 3 4 5 6 7 8 9 10

48. *Variety of Experience*. Sometimes staying in flow requires changing things a bit to vary the experience and keep it fresh. Such variety may include changing plays in a sport, working from another office, taking a new trail in the woods, or a new route to work.

Are you able to generate enough variety in your flow activity to stay interested?

1 2 3 4 5 6 7 8 9 10

49. *Feedback from the Activity Itself*. Without feedback, no system can make corrections to its current path. Persistent and ongoing feedback allows vital information to inform our actions.

As you consider your flow arena, think about the amount and type of feedback you receive and how it affects the quality of your experience. Consider how you notice if you are on the right track or wrong track. Can you tell by score, by feel, by statistic, by outcome, by reaction, or by some other means?

How well do you obtain and implement feedback within this flow activity?

1   2   3   4   5   6   7   8   9   10

50. Taking a Break. Being in flow takes energy—and lots of it. No matter what the arena, when you are engaged in something of high value to you, you tend to put everything into the experience. Despite the fact that those in flow can ignore hunger, postpone going to the bathroom, or even do without sleep for long periods, you cannot keep that up forever. You can revitalize yourself by means of brief breaks, time-outs, short walks, healthful snacks and fluids. All may briefly interrupt flow, but ultimately serve the experience.

How effectively do you use breaks or time-outs (every 60-90 minutes) to re-vitalize yourself?

1   2   3   4   5   6   7   8   9   10

51. Determination. Now consider how you manage your emotional status. As you think about your flow arena, consider your ability to maintain intensity and determination. This source of energy is most needed when you're involved in an activity that, while it may have extraordinary value to you, also presents extraordinary challenge.

How well do you maintain your intensity and determination to succeed within this flow arena?

1   2   3   4   5   6   7   8   9   10

Personal Management Strategies

52. Enough Exercise. The next question, though very broad, is designed to raise your awareness of how well you manage your physical self. Are you aerobically fit? Do you work your heart 3-5 times a week? What about resistance training? Not to be forgotten is stretching, that vital practice that keeps the body limber and relaxed. Together these physical practices do much to support flow.

Do you get ample exercise (cardio, weights, stretch) each week?

1 2 3 4 5 6 7 8 9 10

53. Eating Well. Do your eating patterns support your physical systems and contribute to a high energy level? Your diet ought to be balanced, including minimal fatty foods, small healthy snacks every few hours for consistent energy, and several cups of water daily. Portions need to be reasonable, and alcohol use reasonable.

Rate the quality of your food intake. Are you eating a healthy and balanced diet?

1 2 3 4 5 6 7 8 9 10

54. Rest and Recovery. Plenty of rest and sufficient recovery time are essential to anyone wishing to channel energy towards meaningful ends. Yet day in and day out, I hear—especially from students—"I'm getting so much done, but I didn't get to sleep until 4:30 a.m." Dragging themselves out of bed at 9:00 a.m. or so, they find their way to class and proceed to miss the bulk of their lecture. Many of us have similar patterns and fail to get the required 6-8 hours of sleep that most bodies demand to fully engage everyday.

Do you get enough hours of sleep and sufficient rest and recovery breaks each day to maintain your energy?

1 2 3 4 5 6 7 8 9 10

55. *General Health*. Any significant health issue, if not dealt with, can be a significant distraction and detract from flow. Consider your overall health and wellness for a moment.

To what degree do you rate your overall health and wellness?

1   2   3   4   5   6   7   8   9   10

56. *Personal Needs*. Part of setting the stage for peak performance is doing the little things that make you feel grounded and at ease. Giving attention to your personal needs runs the gamut from getting massages, spending time with friends or family, enjoying the park, to getting a pedicure, or whatever else makes you feel good and gives you that extra sense of satisfaction and personal control.

Do you take care of all of your personal needs, such as time with friends, time for fun, and so on?

1   2   3   4   5   6   7   8   9   10

57. *Living a Balanced Life*. Real-estate author Robert Allen spoke about "the speed of going slow," which is about putting too much energy into any one thing. Consider the father who works 70 hours per week for a larger paycheck, compromising his relationship with family and friends; the athlete who discovers that too much time on the playing field can actually increase his fear of winning and losing because there is too much pressure; or the obsessive gamer whose work suffers. An over-focus on any one activity is unhealthy and counter-productive. High focus and the ability to excel in any one thing often require a sense of balance and harmony.

To what degree do you live a balanced life?

1   2   3   4   5   6   7   8   9   10

58. *Learning from Mistakes*. Some people are better at the learning process than others. Have you witnessed a time when either you or someone else repeated the same error without the awareness to learn and grow from the situation? Insight into our experiences is a vital part of not only our ongoing course correction, but also long-term development.

How well do you learn from each flow experience and use it to prepare for your next flow experience?

1 2 3 4 5 6 7 8 9 10

59. *Mastering your Craft*. Do you actively seek knowledge, new insights, and concepts in your flow arena? Think about your flow arena and ask yourself:

To what degree do you consider yourself a student of your craft—a student of peak performance?

1 2 3 4 5 6 7 8 9 10

60. *Commitment to Excellence*. The final question relates to how committed you are. Those who quest after flow do so at various intensities. There are the casual flow seekers—those who want to be a bit more absorbed and to enjoy their experiences more. And there are those who look at flow as a barometer for increased understanding of their nature and potential. These individuals give everything they have to discover what they are made of, constantly looking for new and innovative ways to take their game—their flow arena—to the next level.

What is your overall commitment to reaching your full potential?

1 2 3 4 5 6 7 8 9 10

More Flow Assets and Liabilities?

A flow asset is a principle that contributes to your flow experience. As I look around at my immediate environment—my home office—I see a variety of flow assets that help me stay focused on the moment. In particular, my desk is organized, the floor is clean, I have a beautiful view, it is quiet, and I am comfortable.

In contrast, flow liabilities derail your flow and challenge your ability to focus. Such was the case several weeks ago when I returned from the Middle East. When I fly, I am usually successful at putting together my strategies for entering flow. I pre-organize my time, identify my goals for each segment of the flight, and rotate the activities to include much variety, I wear comfortable clothing, and generally I have enough sustenance to insure that my concentration will not be broken due to thirst or hunger. However, with a 30-hour flight, this takes a fair amount of effort. Ten hours, no problem. But 30, it's a challenge. In this case the cabin was hot, my back was tight, and I was highly fatigued. Taken together, these factors made it difficult to stay focused on anything. These were liabilities to my flow experience and ones that I will seek to make adjustments for the next time I find myself on a 30-hour transport. While each of these variables are mentioned in the Finding Your Flow Self-Analysis, one specific strategy stood out as an asset. The strategy: noise-cancelling headphones.

While perhaps not a mainstream strategy for all flow seekers, this asset proved quite valuable within a particular arena of mine. Thus, consider similar little strategies that assist you in finding your own flow. What additional, more personal, factors came to mind that impact (either positively or negatively) your own state of flow? Maybe on your Ferrari you have a special spoiler, a lighter frame, a higher grade of fuel, some secret weapon that gives you a unique strength. Or maybe you are dragging an extra 50 pounds of weight, your tires aren't balanced, or your radiator has a leak.

In the spaces below, take just a few minutes to identify any other Flow Assets and Liabilities that might be relevant to your 720-degree sweep:

61._____?

   1   2   3   4   5   6   7   8   9   10

62._____?

   1   2   3   4   5   6   7   8   9   10

63._____?

   1   2   3   4   5   6   7   8   9   10

64._____?

   1   2   3   4   5   6   7   8   9   10

65._____?

   1   2   3   4   5   6   7   8   9   10

Step 2: Identifying Your Flow Assets and Liabilities

Let us now take some time to sort through your self-analysis. Below you will find two sides to this process. The side on the left represents those factors that contribute to your flow experiences. Such factors might include having a clear vision for a particular outcome, an organized workspace, a positive attitude, high physical energy, and the like. This list represents your Flow Assets. Given how you have rated yourself on each of the questions above, list all your #10 ratings, based on the question tags above, such as "Eat well." By definition, these are your greatest Flow Assets.

Follow this by transferring each of your #9 ratings, and so on, until you fill up the page. Note that when you make this transfer, you may have no #10s or #9s. If this is the case, start with your highest numbers and work your way down.

Take at least 10 minutes to complete this exercise so that it represents what you truly believe to be your greatest Flow Assets within the particular arena you are assessing.

Flow Contributors/Assets   Flow Inhibitors/Liabilities

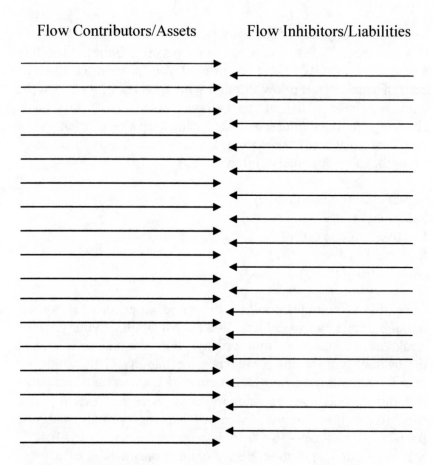

With your greatest Flow Assets listed, it is now time to rate each strength within each number category. For example, let's say you have five strengths you've rated as #10, such as:

Organizing Your Resources (10)
Rest and Recovery (10)
Positive Attitude (10)
Now Focused (10)
Self-Belief (10)

Then take this list and sort them by their relative strength within this category. You may then rate your #10s using a second number list starting with 10 once again. Therefore if you decided that your absolute most valuable flow asset was having Intrinsic

Motivation for your chosen activity, this would be your #10/#10. If your second most valuable asset was Self-Belief, then this would be your #10/#9 and so on until you have sorted through each of your #10s. Follow through with your list of #9s, as well, until you have a list of assets rated by value. If this takes changing numbers around or re-assessing the value of each, that's fine. Just do what it takes to rank your Flow Assets in order of strength, value or perceived impact.

Intrinsic Motivation (10/10)
Self-Belief (10/9)
Positive Attitude (10/8)
Rest and Recovery (10/7)
Now Focused (10/6)

Once this is complete, follow the same procedure for sorting through your Flow Liabilities. Make a list of all of your greatest weaknesses (your #1s), followed by your #2s, and so on. Then list by rank your greatest weakness or liability. This would be your #1/#1, followed by #1/#2, then #1/#3, etc. You'll recognize that this second number category is the reverse of rating your strengths, in that going down from 10s displays small shades of liability or weakness (#10/#10 is a greater asset than #10/#9). Starting from 1 and adding numbers demonstrates small shades of asset (#1/#1 is a greater liability than #1/#2).

Personal Needs (1,1)
Living a Balanced Life (1,2)
Eating Right/Eating Well (1,3)
Self-Confidence (1,4)
Tools & Resources (1,5)

Your more comprehensive list should look something like this:

Flow Arena: Office

Flow Assets	Flow Liabilities
Intrinsic Motivation (10/10)	Personal Needs (1/1)
Self-Belief (10/9)	Living a Balanced Life (1/2)
Positive Attitude (10/8)	Eating Right/Eating Well (1/3)
Rest and Recovery (10/7)	Self-Confidence (1/4)
Now Focused (10/6)	Tools & Resources (1/5)
Feedback form the Activity Itself (9/10)	Comparing Self to Others (2/1)
Excellent Staff (9/9) (additional)	Sense of Humor (2/2)
Tools and Resources (9/8)	Unattractive Workspace (2/3) (additional)
Support from Others (9/7)	Learning from Mistakes (2/4)
Working from Home (9/6) (additional)	Unclear Expectations (2/5) (additional)

Notice that, while you *could* rank each and every variable discussed, there wasn't room to list and rank them all. Most likely you didn't consider anything much lower than 10 or 9 on your Assets list and 1 or 2 on your Liabilities list, as everything in-between is of less value and leverage. This initiates a new shift in focus for you, a narrowing of your attention to those things that matter most. These are what we will pay attention to from now on in this analysis.

Step 3. Building Your Personal Flow Formula

As we emerge from our discussion of Flow Assets and Liabilities, the formula itself becomes a simple form of division where:

$$\text{Flow} = \frac{\text{Flow Assets}}{\text{Flow Liabilities}}$$

If we were to take this simple formula and draw it out even further, we might separate Internal Assets from External Assets, then Internal Liabilities from External Liabilities:

$$\text{Flow} = \frac{\text{Internal Flow Assets} + \text{External Flow Assets}}{\text{Internal Flow Liabilities} + \text{External Flow Liabilities}}$$

Or

$$F = \frac{IA + EA}{IL + EL}$$

To begin the process of narrowing down which factors make our formula, it makes sense to narrow down our lists to a more reasonable number—let's say our top 10 in both the numerator (Internal and External Flow Assets) and the denominator (Internal and External Flow Liabilities). If we were to transfer each of our Flow Assets and each of our Flow Liabilities (both lists sorted accurately based on the numbers we gave them) into this formula, it would look something like this.

$$
\text{Flow} = \frac{\begin{array}{ll} \textbf{Internal Assets} \quad + & \textbf{External Assets} \\ \text{Intrinsic Motivation} & \text{Excellent Staff} \\ \text{Self Belief} & \text{Tools \& Resources} \\ \text{Positive Attitude} & \text{Support from Others} \\ \text{Rest \& Recovery} & \text{Working from Home} \\ \text{Now Focused} \\ \text{Feedback from the Activity Itself} \end{array}}{\begin{array}{ll} \textbf{Internal Liabilities} \quad + & \textbf{External Liabilities} \\ \text{Personal Needs} & \text{Comparing Self to Others} \\ \text{Living a Balanced Life} & \text{Sense of Humor} \\ \text{Eating Right/Eating Well} & \text{Unattractive Workspace} \\ \text{Self-Confidence} & \text{Learning from Mistakes} \\ \text{Tools \& Resources} & \text{Unclear Expectations} \end{array}}
$$

So where do all of the other factors go that don't make your formula? Basically they reside on a "parking lot" list—a list that is neither engaged nor disengaged. They are simply a reference for the future. Here comes the great sigh of relief. You don't have to change everything—just the most important things—even "the one thing!"

Throughout this self-assessment, you have been pondering the many factors that contribute to and take away from flow. Through this 720-degree sweep you have pushed the boundaries of your awareness to be as broad as possible—looking broadly on the inside as well as looking broadly on the outside to determine what works, what doesn't work, what could work, what won't work. Now it's time to take a break from thinking about those things that either you already do relatively well or at least don't cause you significant angst. Shifting from a broad to a narrow focus will help define your great leverage points for personal change and for engineering your flow experience.

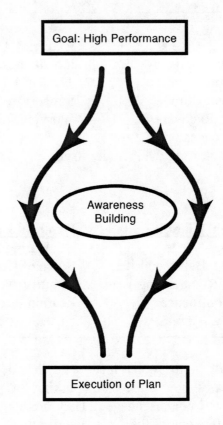

Clarifying the Vital Factors Test

Moving from a broad to a narrow focus means placing your time, energy, and resources, not on everything, but on the most important things. Why should you do this? Why not simply divvy up your time and spend a little bit on several different strategies? The answer can be found in the Pareto Principle named after the famed economist Vilfredo Pareto and made popular by management guru Joseph Juran.

Sometimes known as the 80/20 principle, this principle helps us understand the power of choosing wisely where to focus our resources. Stemming from the observation that 20% of Italians owned 80% of the country's wealth, this concept represents the idea that things are often unevenly distributed. More examples:

120

- 20% of the population pay at least 80% of the taxes
- 20% of the sales force produce at least 80% of the revenue
- 20% of the glitches in cars create at least 80% of the crashes
- 20% of the customers represent 80% of the revenue
- 20% of the athletes will score at least 80% of the points
- 20% of what you spend your time on gives you 80% of your result

Such a list might continue with examples that provide an even starker contrast, such as the fact that, in the United States, 1% of the population pays approximately 40% of the taxes.

This Pareto principle demonstrates the power of focus and the significance of being selective where you place your time, energy and resources. Because of a diminishing marginal benefit, you can spend additional resources on something and get a minimal result. Therefore placing your energies on the right thing for the right amount of time is a significant strategy in and of itself.

In their book, *Influencer*, Patterson, Grenny, Maxfield, McMillan and Switzler do a superb job of discussing the practical realities of influence and change. Whether they are writing about personal, interpersonal, organizational, or societal change, the common theme throughout the book is the power of focusing on the two or three things that produce the greatest result. Whether you're trying to achieve weight loss, modify the behavior of convicted killers, or eradicate the Guinea worm in Africa, amongst the thousands of potential strategies that could be used, a very short list actually produces the needed influence to create the desired change.

It all boils down to simplicity. It's not a hundred things you need to do to improve your life, feel happier, or find your flow. It's only a few key changes that will make the bulk of the difference. The fact is, however, it's not just any two or three things, it's *your* two or three things.

This brings us back to our process for sorting through all of the factors that in some way affect your flow experience.

At this point in my workshops, when I ask participants to share their #1#1 (their greatest Flow Liability) and #10#10 (their greatest Flow Asset), the group can't help but notice that nearly everyone in the room has a different #1#1 and #10#10. Some themes, though, do invariably show up again and again. Some people describe their lack of vision, others struggle with managing time. Many are challenged to stay focused, eat well, get enough exercise, manage emotions, stay organized, and so on. When you go through this process, you begin to gather new and valuable insights into the nature of your experiences. Most importantly, you develop a better understanding of what works for you. The process takes you from being unconsciously incompetent to a new state of conscious incompetence—that wonderful state of awareness that sets the stage for making new commitment towards important changes.

Three Ways to Increase Flow

With your refined Personal Flow Formula in place, you are now ready to choose the single factor that is the most important to you right now and build a plan around it.

Let's think about simple division problems. In school, you may have learned (and forgotten) that there are essentially three ways to increase a sum. The first is to add something to the numerator. This would mean taking a current Flow Asset and deciding to strengthen it, add to it, or sustain it in a more profound way. For instance, if one of your Flow Assets is high physical energy because this sustains you through your moments of flow performance, then you would make sure to build ample routines to insure that this strength stays high. This may include getting ample sleep each night, eating small meals six times per day to sustain your sugar levels, or taking short breaks every hour or so. If a high internal Flow Asset is your intrinsic motivation, then you may choose to reflect on the purpose of your work from time to time to reinforce those positive feelings, which tap into deeper forms of energy.

A second way to increase flow is to look at the denominator in the division problem and review your Flow Liabilities. To increase flow you must decrease a liability. For instance, if one of your Flow Liabilities is being constantly interrupted, you might seek reasonable ways to decrease such interruptions. These may include developing practical strategies such as closing an office door, turning off your phone, learning to apply the 80/20 rule to everything you do, arranging times during the day when you have fewer distractions, and so on. If you struggle to manage your time and are usually late for appointments, you may choose to use a planning system to hold yourself accountable for each segment of the day.

A third and the most powerful way to increase your flow is to once again focus on the denominator, but instead of simply decreasing a Flow Liability, you actually turn a liability into an asset. For example, take the strategy of inner dialogue or self-talk. Perhaps you find yourself in situations where your attitude is self-defeating. You may be critical of yourself, making statements to yourself that squander your focus and contribute to performance problems. Let's say that you have become aware of this habit pattern and wish to modify your beliefs and attitudes by working on your internal dialogue. What you do, then, is notice when such trains of thought begin and take time to re-define your language, using more positive language to describe the situation. Through this change, your attitude, emotional climate, demeanor, and confidence would all begin to increase. Then you would start seeing yourself not only as a less pessimistic thinker, but as a convert to a new more positive paradigm of thinking, feeling and behaving.

Such changes are possible if you make a concerted effort to convert ways of life that are liabilities into a more productive train of positive behaviors. Take the case of a highly stressed stockbroker who becomes a master at deep relaxation, an attorney who skillfully manages negative emotions, a firefighter who learns to stay focused during a large fire, a teenager who finds intrinsic motivation for learning calculus, or a doctor who develops new systems of organization that allow for greater efficiency. Given that most of the factors we have been discussing are highly learnable and not simply inherited talents, we have practically unlimited capacities to change and evolve in directions that are most important to us.

Let's look at the math. Let's assume for the moment that we have twice the number of Flow Assets as we do Flow Liabilities. Now let's play with the numbers and see how manipulating the numerator or the denominator changes the outcome:

$$2 = \frac{100}{50}$$

Strategy 1: Increasing a strength by 20 units

$$2.4 = \frac{120}{50}$$

Strategy 2: Decreasing a weakness by 20 units

$$3.3 = \frac{100}{30}$$

Strategy 3: Decreasing a weakness by 20 units and turning it into 20 units of strength

$$4 = \frac{120}{30}$$

As you can see, either action contributes to the overall result, but decreasing a liability, even turning that liability into a strength has the greatest impact on performance. Using the simple formulas above, by adding 20 points to your Flow Assets, you increase the probability of flow by 20 per cent. Decreasing your Flow Liabilities by 20 points will increase your probability of flow by 70 per cent. Decreasing your Flow Liabilities number by 20 and transferring these points into the Flow Asset numerator increases the probability of flow by 100 per cent. This is a nice reward for removing the interference and putting in place a new factor, practice, or habit that directly contributes to your flow. While it's clear that anywhere you choose to spend your time and resources will help you raise your ability to find flow, spending time in the Flow Liabilities camp has the potential for even greater results.

Section IV: Planning, Executing & Learning

CHAPTER 9: Action Planning for Flow

Through this journey towards flow, we have moved from Unconscious Incompetence (not knowing that you don't know) to a new level of Conscious Incompetence (now knowing that you don't know). We have recognized, after conducting our 720-degree sweep, that the bulk of the factors related to flow probably don't need much personal attention right now. Instead, only one or two issues need to be the focus of our attention.

Now is the time to become intentional. By narrowing your focus internally you are making a conscious decision to exclude less important flow factors to THE most important one (or two). You will then focus externally for new methods, strategies or practices that will help you become more consciously competent in putting more flow in your life. So let's do just that.

In the space below, identify the "one thing" that will be the focus of your attention over the next 30-90 days. Remember, you can either choose to advance or sustain a current Flow Asset or remove a Flow Liability—or one of each if you choose.

The most important change I can make in the next 30-90 days is:

The second most important change I can make in the next 30-90 days is:

Setting SMART Goals to Increase Flow

Now that you have identified the focus of your training journey, you will want to clarify that focus in a meaningful way. It's one thing to identify a developmental area, yet another to define it in such a way that you become clear about exactly what actions you're going to take.

One of the most effective means of clarifying your goal is to make sure that it meets certain criteria—let's call it the SMART criteria—a kind of gauntlet to put your goals through in order to translate good intentions into firm reality. SMART stands for setting goals that are Specific, Meaningful yet Measurable, Aggressive yet Realistic, and Time-sensitive. For example, if you have found that your greatest challenge is managing your time, it is not enough to set a goal that says: Improve time management skills. Such a notion is too nebulous. Instead, let's take this same intention and make it SMART.

Such a conversion might look like this: Over the next 60 days I will purchase a daily planner and spend 15 minutes planning and preparing my calendar for each day. This goal is more specific and meaningful because it's your "one thing," it's measurable (planning for 15 minutes each day), it's aggressive yet realistic (it should be pushing your limits but not thwarting your resolve to complete it), and it's time-sensitive (a habit to be completed within 60 days). By making your goals SMART, you greatly increase your odds of success.

Consider the following sample SMART goals as you craft your own:
1. Read one new book this month on strategies to improve personal organization.
2. Practice deep breathing through meditation for 20 minutes each day for 30 days.
3. Spend 10 minutes each morning planning a daily calendar.

4. Drink 64 ounces of water every day for a month.
5. Proactively ask for feedback from a close friend at least once per week. Then summarize strengths and weaknesses for the next two weeks.

Using the worksheet below, write down your goal and assess how well you crafted it using the SMART criteria:

Flow Strategy Development

Now that you have identified your most important Flow Asset and Liability, develop one SMART strategy for either or both sides of the equation. Remember, a SMART goal/strategy is one that is Specific (S), Measurable (M), Aggressive (A), Realistic (R), and Time-specific (T).

Largest Flow Asset: **Largest Flow Liability:**

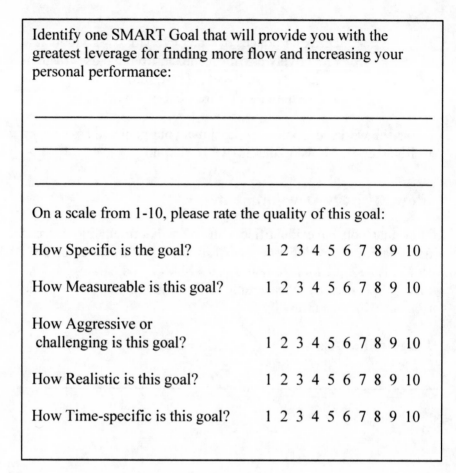

Identify one SMART Goal that will provide you with the greatest leverage for finding more flow and increasing your personal performance:

_____

_____

_____

On a scale from 1-10, please rate the quality of this goal:

How Specific is the goal?   1 2 3 4 5 6 7 8 9 10

How Measureable is this goal?   1 2 3 4 5 6 7 8 9 10

How Aggressive or
challenging is this goal?   1 2 3 4 5 6 7 8 9 10

How Realistic is this goal?   1 2 3 4 5 6 7 8 9 10

How Time-specific is this goal?   1 2 3 4 5 6 7 8 9 10

Now that you have identified one SMART strategy on one or both sides of your Personal Flow Formula, strive to develop Conscious Competence—or even Unconscious Competence within each area. Once you have developed a successful habit or behavior, begin looking at the next largest Flow Asset and Liability and generate SMART goals and strategies for your next phase of development.

As you continue this process of self-awareness, analysis, planning, execution, evaluation, and habit formation, you will build a more comprehensive personal formula for finding more flow, high performance and personal effectiveness in any one of your MLAs.

With your SMART goal, or goals (if you want to address a second developmental area at the same time) in place, it is vital that you take the necessary steps to insure your commitment for change. At this point one critical strategy has already been achieved: writing your goals(s) down. It is now a tangible and written contract with yourself—one that you should keep with you every day. Whether it's on paper or a PDA or other electronic device, it doesn't matter. What does matter is that you review your goal(s) often to keep your vision clear in your mind.

Holding Yourself Accountable: Coaching Yourself to Success

Now that you've identified your main goal or goals and determined a path of action, you are ready to identify a clear strategy for holding yourself accountable. Essential for your success is a tracking system that will help you measure your progress through your journey of personal change. No matter how vital and clear your goals are, there are still a million and one ways to *not* accomplish what you set out to do. Excuses always abound, no matter how well intentioned you are. The remedy: personal accountability.

Personal accountability suggests that you *count* something, which happens to be one of the vital aspects of SMART goal setting. Remember, vagueness is the death of objective. Take, for instance, swimmer Florence Chaddick, the first woman ever to swim the English Channel both ways. In 1952 she set a goal to swim to Catalina Island off the coast of California. With her goal clearly set, she had everything in place to meet her objective, including a support team, even shooters to keep the sharks away from her in the frigid waters. But dense fog kept her from seeing the land she was swimming toward. Florence had no way of measuring her progress and ultimately asked to be pulled from the water. The travesty: she was only a half-mile from the shoreline. She ultimately achieved her goal, however, beating the men's record by more than two hours. Yet her first attempt was thwarted by a lack of feedback and of the ability to measure herself against her end goal.[54]

Lesson: It is extremely difficult to manage one's body, thoughts and emotions without information for maintaining perspective and charting progress towards the end goal.

Remember: What gets measured gets done. So let's discuss for a moment what it means to measure and track your progress.

No objective was ever achieved by simply creating some sort of mission statement and then writing down the goal. That's only the plan, and the plan must be actualized. Perhaps you've decided to work on your Flow Liability of being tired throughout the day. You realize that this needs to change if you are to be fully engaged. There are a few ways you can address this issue. After careful consideration, perhaps reading a few articles or a book on the subject of sleep, you identify a few of the most obvious strategies: simply getting more sleep (whatever your own optimal amount is), or taking a short nap in the afternoon (20-30 minutes). You decide to begin by converting your current 4-5 hour habit into a 6-8 hour habit. To keep yourself accountable, you can build a simple chart or scorecard.

Tracking the process of sleep is quite basic, and you can use whatever tool you would like—a piece of paper or something more complex like an Excel spreadsheet. If your goal is to get a minimum of 7 hours per night over the next 30 days and your expected outcome is to feel more energy throughout the day, you are now clear on both the process (number of hours of sleep) and the outcome (perceived increase in energy). You are now ready to chart your daily progress.

To put together a process number, use whatever tool you have chosen to draw 30 horizontal lines across the paper (one line per day). Then in two columns on the top of the sheet write "Process Measure" and next to it "Outcome Measure." You already know your process measurement system: counting hours of sleep. In the

"Process Measure" column you simply write a 6, 7, 8 for however many hours you slept the night before. The outcome measure is a little less exact. You might choose to rate how you feel at the end of each day, using any scale you wish, such as 1-10 or 1-100. If you choose a 1-10 scale you might rate 1 as feeling very tired and lethargic vs. 10, which would mean you feel highly alert and energetic. Each day for 30 days, you can write down how many hours you slept followed by how much energy you felt during the day. Over time, say 30-90 days, you can draw a simple correlation between the time you slept and how it impacted your energy. Such a chart might look like this:

Date	Process Measure (sleep hours)	Outcome Measure (energy level)
6/1	4	50
6/2	5	60
6/3	6	70
6/4	7	80
6/5	8	100
6/6	7	80
6/7	8	90
6/8	7	80
6/9	7	80
6/10	7	80
6/11	8	100
6/12	8	100
6/13	8	100
6/14	9	100
6/15	9	100
6/16	8	100
6/17	8	100
6/18	6	70
6/19	8	100
6/20	8	100
6/21	7	90
6/22	8	100
6/23	8	100

6/24	8	100
6/25	8	100
6/26	8	100
6/27	8	100
6/28	8	100
6/29	8	100
6/30	8	100

Here you can see a simple correlation between sleep and energy level so that with each additional hour of sleep you get, your energy increases. This charting system not only provides a simple method for gathering feedback and seeing a connection between effort and outcome, it forces you to be accountable to yourself daily. You are also building up a daily habit that, over a 30-90 day period, you can expect to become effortlessly ingrained into your daily behavior.

More advanced methods of keeping track may give you even more support, along with a more visual display of your progress. Let's take a deeper look at a measurement system that takes personal accountability to the next level.

This scorecarding system has a variety of tools to help you stay focused and accountable. Let's review each, starting from the top of the page and working our way down.

Example 1: Deep breathing and pre-visualizing your day (a direct flow enhancement strategy).

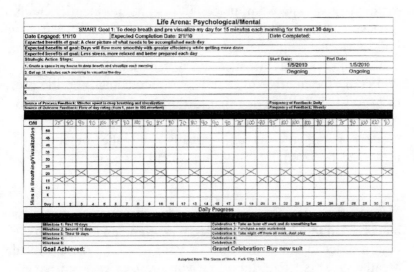

Life Arena: Psychological/Mental

SMART Goal 1: To deep breath and pre visualize my day for 15 minutes each morning for the next 30 days

| Date Engaged: 1/1/10 | Expected Completion Date: 2/1/10 | Date Completed: |

Expected benefits of goal: A clear picture of what needs to be accomplished each day
Expected benefits of goal: Days will flow more smoothly with greater efficiency while getting more done
Expected benefits of goal: Less stress, more relaxed and better prepared each day

Strategic Action Steps:	Start Date:	End Date:
1. Create a space in my house to deep breath and visualize each morning	1/5/2010	1/5/2010
2. Get up 15 minutes each morning to visualize the day	Ongoing	Ongoing
3		
4		
5		
6		

Source of Process Feedback: Minutes spent in deep breathing and visualization — Frequency of Feedback: Daily
Source of Outcome Feedback: Flow of day rating (from 1, poor to 100 excellent) — Frequency of Feedback: Weekly

Milestone 1: First 10 days — Celebration 1: Take an hour off work and do something fun
Milestone 2: Second 10 days — Celebration 2: Purchase a new audiobook
Milestone 3: Third 10 days — Celebration 3: Take night off from all work. Just play
Milestone 4: — Celebration 4:
Milestone 5: — Celebration 5:
Goal Achieved: — **Grand Celebration: Buy new suit**

At the top of the page, we first identify the life arena that we are choosing to work within, "Psychological/Mental" in this instance. Next, using the SMART criteria, we state our goal as: To deep breathe and pre-visualize my day for 15 minutes each morning for 30 days. We declare the beginning date of this goal as 1/1 and that we expect to complete the goal by 2/1.

To clarify why you want to proceed, you can write down the expected benefits of achieving this goal. This calls upon the intrinsically-motivated energy that will keep you on task. In this example, the benefits of pre-visualizing your day are that it helps you develop a clearer picture of what needs to be accomplished, a more smoothly flowing day with greater efficiency, all while getting more done with less stress and much better preparation. Of course, there are dozens of other benefits you can list.

Next, in preparation for achieving this goal, you may determine that several strategic action steps are necessary, such as creating a space at home to deep breathe and visualize daily. Also you can set your alarm and plan to get up 15 minutes early each morning. This is an ongoing strategic action step.

With your pre-steps in place, it is time to identify both the process measure (what you do) and the outcome measure (what you get) that will help you track your progress. For pre-visualizing your day the measure is very simple. Most likely you will count the number of minutes you are actually in the process of pre-visualizing. Notice that in this example both your process measure and your outcome measure are charted daily with the process being measured vertically and the outcome being measured horizontally. Both are quantitative, yet the process is also visual so you can see your progress.

Your goal is to see a correlation between your actions and your outcome. In this case you are deep breathing and visualizing your day in order to affect the flow of your day. The more your deep breathe and visualize, the more you are expecting to have your day flow smoothly. If this is not the case you will want to re-consider what you are measuring until you find a process that works for the outcome you desire.

Once you are on track and moving in the right direction, begin setting milestones and mini-victories on the way towards goal completion. Here the goal was broken into three mini-goals with three distinct external rewards to drive motivation. The first was the first 10 days of action, at which point an hour off work was set as the mini-reward. The second 10 days prompted the purchase of an audio book. The reward for the third and final 10 days was to take a night off work and just play, with the grand celebration being the purchase of a new suit. Of course these rewards can be anything you wish, but they should be an additional motivation tool for you—something you truly look forward to and will help prompt your daily, weekly, even monthly actions.

Example 2: Weight loss
(an indirect flow enhancement strategy)

Let's consider a more indirect strategy for finding flow, a health habit that most of us struggle with at some point in our lives— weight loss. A scorecarding method can prove very useful in conjunction with other proven weight-loss strategies.

At the top of the page, we first identify the life arena that we are choosing to work within, "Physical" in this instance. Next, using the SMART criteria, we state our goal as: To lose 10 pounds in 60 days. We declare the beginning date of this goal as 1/1 and that we expect to complete the goal by 3/1.

To clarify why you want to proceed, write down the expected benefits. This calls upon the intrinsically motivated energy that will keep you on task. In this example, the benefits of losing 10 pounds include the following: demonstrating a sense of self-control, easing back pressure, and improving the fit of clothes. Of course, there are dozens of other benefits such as improved stamina, how you look, lower cholesterol, etc. Declaring the benefits that are most meaningful to you helps keep you motivated.

Next, in preparation for achieving this goal, you may determine that several strategic action steps are necessary, such as purchasing a gym membership and getting up an hour early each day.

Once your pre-steps are in place, identify both the process measure (what you do) and the outcome measure (what you get). For weight loss there are many ways to measure progress. A process measure may include counting calories, minutes or hours of exercise, total weights lifted in a workout, steps taken per day, and so on. In this example, aerobic minutes per day are counted with the expectation that this will lead to losing weight. Notice that in this example the frequency of measurement is daily, but the outcome measure is weekly and is noted at the top of the chart. You can just as easily measure your outcome daily or by any frequency you deem appropriate.

With this system, you not only measure your process and outcome, but you can see your progress visually, with process measures in the vertical columns daily and outcome measures in the vertical columns weekly. The peaks and the valleys of your efforts are viewable.

If you see a direct correlation (in this case, if you see that each week in which you increase your exercise, your weight goes down), you know that you're on the right track. Otherwise, you will want to re-consider what you are measuring until you find a process that works.

For any of your goals, there is most likely a body of knowledge out there that you would benefit from becoming familiar with. Losing weight and keeping it off, for example, is a multi-billion dollar industry, and no one method is right for everyone. If you take some time to learn a bit of the science around the change you seek, you can put a plan in place that will be more likely to lead to your goal.

Identifying the Right Measure

Take once again the example of weight loss. It is a common goal to lose 10 or more pounds. Often, however, individuals are given not only new strategies for managing food intake (another goal to measure) but also for exercise methods. These often include both aerobic (rapid heart rate) exercises mixed with resistance training (lifting weights). If this combination of strategies is part of your regimen and you decide to measure your aerobic minutes per day and weekly progress towards weight loss, you may be disappointed, not because you aren't making progress, but because your measuring system may not be giving you the whole story. Certainly you may be losing fat and excess weight, but because of your resistance training (which does more to burn fat than any other strategy) you may actually be gaining weight.

What kind of weight? Muscle weight. This is a good thing, yet your outcome number may not be going in the direction that you thought it would. The solution: change what you measure.

In this case your real goal may be to lose body fat with the added benefit of gaining a stronger, more toned body. But your original goal may have been to lean up and burn off excess fat. In this case you may still count as your process the number of aerobic minutes per day, or even the total number of minutes per day that you are in work-out mode. However, instead of measuring weight loss (through a simple scale) you measure decrease in body fat— a completely different measure which more accurately measures progress towards your end goal.

Let's say, for instance that you have a body-fat index of 32%—a simple measure that you can have taken at most gyms. Your new goal may be to decrease that number to 20%. With this new measurement system in place, you once again measure your process but this time seek a new measure—one that will truly mark your progress. If you have set a goal that goes beyond a 30-day time period, perhaps towards a 2-3 month time period, then you can continue your charting using a simpler graph like the one below:

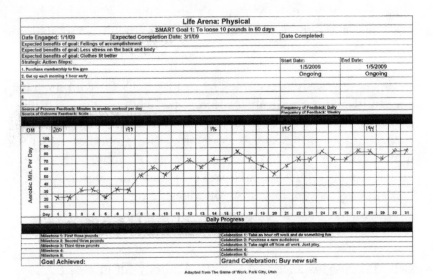

Life Arena: Physical

SMART Goal 1: To loose 10 pounds in 60 days

Date Engaged: 1/1/09	Expected Completion Date: 3/1/09	Date Completed:	
Expected benefits of goal: Feelings of accomplishment			
Expected benefits of goal: Less stress on the back and body			
Expected benefits of goal: Clothes fit better			
Strategic Action Steps:		Start Date:	End Date:
1. Purchase membership to the gym		1/5/2009	1/5/2009
2. Get up each morning 1 hour early		Ongoing	Ongoing
3			
4			
5			
6			
Source of Process Feedback: Minutes in aerobic workout per day		Frequency of Feedback: Daily	
Source of Outcome Feedback: Scale		Frequency of Feedback: Weekly	

Milestone 1: First three pounds	Celebration 1: Take an hour off work and do something fun
Milestone 2: Second three pounds	Celebration 2: Purchase a new audiobook
Milestone 3: Third three pounds	Celebration 3: Take night off from all work. Just play.
Milestone 4:	Celebration 4:
Milestone 5:	Celebration 5:
Goal Achieved:	**Grand Celebration: Buy new suit**

Adapted from The Game of Work, Park City, Utah

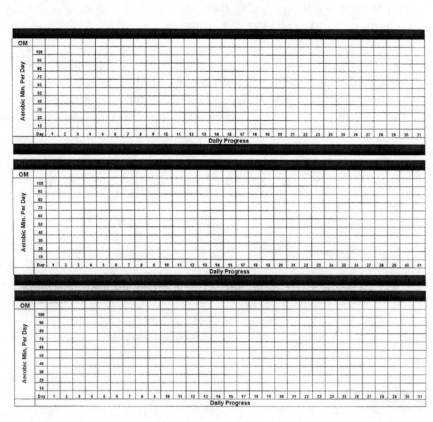

Not every goal will have so many options for measurement. Some are more straightforward: number of compliments given out per day (outcome: to find more flow in relationships), number of smiles per day (outcome: to increase happy feelings), number of minutes organizing yourself per day (outcome: to remove immediate distractions), etc.

Becoming Consciously Competent

As you know by now, becoming consciously competent means developing a new skill or pattern of behavior that you now own.

Now that you have come this far in the process, you have undoubtedly identified and crafted your current training objective that will produce the outcome you desire. It is now through the persistent process of applied practice that you will be intentional about developing a new habit pattern—one that you will sustain for the rest of your life.

The trick in all of this is keeping in mind that there is no short-cut to skill- building and habit-formation. There is no special insight that will cut this time in half or make it any easier on you. The question you have to ask yourself is: do I really want the new change in my life? With this question in mind, are you truly committed to the shift in thinking or behavior that will put you in the driver's seat so that you will own this new skill-set, attitude, or behavior?

Anyone can understand the formula for losing weight: fewer calories, regular exercise, daily measurement, etc., but very few stick with the program. Instead they push hard for a short period of time, begin slipping back into old patterns of behavior, and then do more damage to their bodies by gaining more weight and feeling much worse about their lack of self-discipline. Most of us do, to some degree, have set-backs when we seek personal change. However, regardless of these set-backs, your overarching desire for change must prevail.

As you ponder any new training objective and set of goals, you might consider finding a partner to help support you along the way. A partner can help you stay committed and accountable. This doesn't mean that you have to check in with this person every day, though that may indeed be helpful. Simply sharing your written goal with this person may help.

Or instead of merely sharing your goals, you may choose to partner with another person who is equally as committed to a personal change as you are. You can develop a buddy system where you hold each other accountable to complete your goals. As a more social process, it may inspire both you and your partner to "go the distance." Such is the power of the Weight Watchers program that successfully helps people lose weight and keep it off. One of their strategies is building a social component to the process whereby people can talk with one another and support one another in achieving common goals. Such is the focus of most personal change programs that recognize the power of social support and putting together like-minded people. However, only you know whether you would benefit from working with a social support partner.

It is through persistent application and practice, whether by yourself or with others, that you ultimately develop that wonderful state called Unconscious Competence—in essence, a new habit. With several months of new behavior or thinking patterns in place, your mind and body have now taken them on as part of your normal daily repertoire. The habits and attitudes are now something you own, not only consciously, but unconsciously.

Cases in Personal Change

Now I will share a few inspiring case histories that I've encountered in my workshops and courses. You may be surprised at what comes out of following the entire Finding Your Flow process.

Gina M.

Gina M. was a young woman who wanted to work on her spiritual life arena. As you may imagine, improving in this area can be somewhat abstract. I asked her what it would look like to her to ultimately become more spiritual. She said it would be directly related to the amount of scriptures that she read. Several ideas for measurement were discussed: minutes of scripture reading per day, number of paragraphs or pages read, number of principles/concepts comprehended, etc. It seemed that measuring the number of principles/concepts comprehended would be the best possible measure for Gina. The other measures were too easy to cheat on and/or it was too easy to focus on time or pages without actually comprehending what was read.

Her goal was to read until a minimum of three principles or concepts were understood each day. Her reading may have taken only a few minutes or as long as an hour, a few paragraphs or a few pages. With this simple process measure in place, it was now our job to identify an outcome measure that would satisfy her need to progress and to become more spiritual. This, again, is a very abstract and difficult idea to measure, but less so if you think of the goal through the lens of quality instead of quantity.

A quality measure is something that you can assess based on your own perception. Such a measure might include how confident you are, how happy, how hungry, how contented, and so on. Gina decided to create a "spirituality index" and give herself a score at the end of each day on how she felt from the spiritual perspective. Her scale was 1-100, where 1 was she felt "extremely non-spiritual" and 100 was "extremely spiritual"— with 50 representing "somewhat spiritual." This is not only a very simple measurement process, but an effective one as it forces the rater to make a judgment call that has personal meaning.

With this system in place Gina was able to hold herself accountable while graphically seeing her progress on her path to spirituality.

Jesse T.

A hyperactive perfectionist with a passion for his career, Jesse T. was a workaholic. Taking a deep look at his family life (his arena for the flow assessment) showed him that finding his flow was contingent upon building a more solid foundation with his family, especially his children. He recognized that no success in the office could compensate for failure in the home. Coming to grips with this awareness left Jesse wondering what he could do to let his family know how much he cared and wished to serve them.

After some deep reflection, Jesse recognized that in addition to spending a minimum of two hours with his family each night after work, there was another time in the day where he could be more connected with his kids: at breakfast. Typically at Jesse's house, his wife made breakfast while the kids watched cartoons. Jesse would be tucked away in his office and well on his second hour of the workday before the kids came downstairs. He decided this was now his time to make a connection. His goal was to make breakfast for his family five days a week. From a strategic standpoint, this meant he would have to get up 45 minutes earlier.

After his goal was set, he explained to his family his intention of spending more quality time with them at breakfast. Then Jesse proceeded to make this a priority in his life and one that he keeps to this day. Jesse was able to create a simple outcome measure such as a "family unity" metric (1, poor relations with family, to 100, exceptional relations with family) and making this happen was rewarding in and of itself. His goal of 20 days a month (when he's in town), has made a significant difference in the lives of his family and in his commitment to serve those who mean the most to him. He achieved more flow for himself and more flow for his family, as well.

Kathy M.

Kathy M., a middle-aged woman interested in improving her health (a more indirect flow strategy), decided it was time to do something about her cholesterol level. Through a variety of health tests that were part of our full course, Kathy discovered that her cholesterol was in the high range and that it was a potential Flow Liability. While it wasn't something that hindered her ability to excel in many of her life arenas, it did weigh on her mind enough to be dealt with before it was too late.

With a cholesterol level around 220, Kathy researched several options that would help her decrease this number. For her it was a matter of replacing certain daily food items: chips, cookies, French fries, etc., and replacing them with more healthful foods. So up front we have a simple starting point: 220. Her SMART Goal: anything under 180 within 90 days.

Kathy identified several food items that she wanted to start consuming, including fruits and vegetables. If she could replace the bad stuff with the good stuff, she understood that this new pattern of behavior would take her out of the red zone and into the green. She decided to measure the number of servings of either fruit or vegetables per day for 30 days. If she ate 3 pieces of fruit and 2 servings of vegetables, then her daily number was a 5.

Over the course of 90 days, Kathy kept a daily log of her intake of fruits and vegetables and watched as her cholesterol number decreased. Of course, eating fruits and veggies is not the only answer to decreasing cholesterol. For most people, exercise is a major factor that should be addressed. For others, prescriptions are necessary. In any case, after consulting a doctor and/or the literature, a personalized plan with clear process and outcome metrics will insure either a successful outcome or at least a clear understanding of what is not working. Recognizing that there are many strategies to achieve the same goal, however, is very important.

Tony S.

A novice piano player, Tony S. wanted to take his skills to the next level. With little structure in his practice routine, Tony decided he wanted to improve his piano playing by tackling some hymns that he wanted to learn to play for his church choir. To find even a little flow in this process, Tony decided to set an outcome goal of mastering 6 hymns in 60 days. To do this, he was going to practice a minimum of 20 minutes per day and rotate the songs so he would not be as likely to get stale or bored.

Tony had a simple process measure of minutes per day of practice and an outcome measure that was a judgment call on his part. He would judge whether he felt competent in playing each song without any errors. Once he could play all 6 without errors, his goal was met.

With such a basic measurement system in place, Tony kept daily track of his progress. He ended up going beyond his original goal and mastering several additional songs as well—a testament to the fact that while sometimes our goals are more challenging than we assume, sometimes we deny ourselves a proper challenge and must raise the bar mid-course.

Neal B.

A mortgage broker, Neal B. knew that one of his areas of weakness was a sloppy and unattractive desk. He discovered that, throughout the day, his lack of organization was causing him to look for papers that he needed to close a particular deal. To find more flow, Neal decided it was time to spend time each day getting more organized and developing strategies to get his work done more quickly and efficiently.

Recognizing that a more advanced filing system might do the trick, Neal picked up two books on various filing and organizing strategies. Neal decided to purchase a desk-top filing system where he could separate his clients by closing date. This was to accompany his general reference filing which was often left to chance.

Neal committed to organizing his files and his desk for 15 minutes each day. This included purchasing a label maker and making his files more presentable and pleasing to look at. His outcome measure was a simple "flow index" (1-100) that he used to rate how smoothly his day went, as he could now find what he was looking for while staying on track with each of his clients . This was a very simple strategy, but one that directly impacted his daily and hourly focus.

Britta W.

Britta was a student who rarely wore a smile on her face. It was a problem for her. As she put it, her "blank stare" affected not only her own emotional state, but that of those she associated with. The problem was impacting her interpersonal flow. She felt that if she could work on her smile, and subsequently the self-talk that accompanied a happier disposition, that this would have a significant impact in her life.

Britta decided that a realistic goal for her was to smile each time she came into direct contact with a friend or loved one. She was to count how many times this took place each day and to keep track of her progress. This was her process: counting smiles or her smiling index. The outcome of this new behavior was expected to generate greater levels of happiness and joy in her life, helping her to connect more deeply with those she associated with. Her outcome measure was a scale of 1-100 indicating her level of connection and interpersonal flow.

Over the course of 90 days Britta used the scorecard to chart her progress. At first her smiles were few, but within weeks the number grew. Smiling at people became easier, even second nature to her. At the end of each day she would indicate her level of connection which continued to rise each week as she continued to build her daily ritual.

According to Britta, through this simple change she was able to initiate more intimate conversations, develop deeper connections, and even more importantly, she just plain felt happier.

Repeating Flow

Consider your new behavioral change for a moment. Let's say that over the past couple of months you identified that your #1 #1 Flow Liability was your inability to manage your time effectively. As such, you went through the process of reading a few books and several current articles on the subject, purchasing a daily planner, and attending a workshop that gave you a new system for personal organization. Instead of waking up each morning and attacking the first project you see, you now actually take the time to review your day, identify the tasks that are most valuable to accomplish. You stick to your system by reviewing your calendar and action lists every hour, which then frees you to stay within the moment, with only brief references needed to keep you on track. After ample practice and habit formation, you no longer have to consciously review your days and hours—you do this process automatically, giving you the freedom to be consciously competent for the bulk of each hour of each day.

After months of this narrow focus and execution where new habit patterns are formed, it is time to cycle back once again to an internal and external broad focus. Here another 720° sweep reveals new Flow Assets and Liabilities that both hinder and assist you in your quest for flow. By carefully reviewing the impact of each of these factors, you once again clarify your #1#1 and #10#10 and so on, until your new personal flow formula reveals itself within the Meaningful Life Arena you are assessing.

Now is a good time to re-visit the most pressing factors from your last 720° sweep —even your parking-lot list which may now be more relevant than it was before. Perhaps after another 720° sweep you find that the very next item that was your #1#2 has risen to the #1#1 spot. However, situations and people change. Perhaps an entirely new set of conditions are present and require a solution that was not on your radar three months ago. Like the Ferrari that has been running at high speeds for several laps around the track, if a strut, tire, or piston finally gives way, your attention will have to be focused on solving that problem.

By re-visiting the questions of the Finding Your Flow Self-Analysis, in addition to developing a broader list of factors that you feel either contribute to or hinder your ability to find flow, you are now once again in a position to narrow your focus and choose a new area of development.

Translating Values into Virtues

As you make use of the Finding Your Flow process over time, you are literally becoming a different person. Each iteration of awareness, decision-making, action-taking, and habit-forming is re-arranging your life—your mind, body, heart, and soul—in the direction of your most important values. Doing this successfully by forming permanent habits doesn't just change your outer or inner reality, it is about changing who you are as a person.

Many people are given credit for this quote: "Sow a thought and you reap an action; sow an act and you reap a habit; sow a habit and you reap a character; sow a character and you reap a destiny." The development of new behaviors and habits, once embedded, become our virtues, our character. In some small way we have added to what God has given us at birth, become something more on our very own. This is the essence of personal growth. These virtues and the authenticity that comes from living these virtues, continue to invite future moments of flow.

SG put it this way:

> When I have been in flow, I am engaged in the moment and the activity for the right reasons. There is integrity in the moment, I am projecting something that is real and not the illusion of something that I am trying to be and that I am not.

BH said:

> Flow is consistent with my values, or who I want
> to be. I have never had a flow experience that
> ultimately proved inconsistent with either of those.

And another person (SS) expressed a similar view:

> Moments of flow are very self-confirming. They
> sustain who I think I am. They are energizing and
> confirming. I get more in tune with who I think I
> am and what I am all about.

At this point you have moved beyond simply valuing this change
in your life. You now own the change. It has now become part of
who you are, or a virtue if you will, allowing you to perform
moment to moment in a more personally relevant way.

I recently sought to develop a positive virtue in my life. After
studying the lives of great men and women, I noticed a common
theme that supported higher levels of performance and flow
throughout their day: getting up early. I wondered what rituals
and practices I had been neglecting because of a lack of time. It
came to me: writing, meditation, morning study (scriptures and
science), and most importantly, spending quality time with my
family. I decided to work all of this together into one large new
behavioral ritual that I knew would have a significant impact in
my own life as well as the life of my family.

I began with the understanding that I would get up at 5:15 a.m.
and begin my day with one hour of writing, followed by 20
minutes of meditation, then 30 minutes of aerobic activity while
reading scriptures and books, followed by making breakfast for
my family. At first it was a struggle, but the idea was compelling.
I knew what each new behavioral pattern would do for me
personally, professionally, spiritually, and for my family. What

was initially a difficult pattern to weave eventually became second nature.

Through this new pattern of morning activities, I began being more productive. I was centering myself for the first time in years, I was getting my body active early in the day, and it gave me a chance to turn off the morning TV and be in front of my family while I made breakfast. This gave us 30 focused minutes per day to talk, connect, and simply be together. What a gift! I have now made this my morning ritual, and it is now mine to keep.

Certainly there are days when I cannot accomplish each of these tasks. Early morning flights and late night meetings sometimes get in the way, but I'm about 90% on target—and it works for me and my family. I find my flow in this process. It serves many of my core values: my health, profession, spiritual growth, but most crucially, serving my wife and children. My life runs more smoothly and my relationships continue to grow and evolve. I'm in my flow because I am paying attention to those things that are the most valuable and critical—leaving all extraneous and low-value tasks out of the picture. My focus is clear.

CHAPTER 10: Becoming Your Own Best Coach

Before we close this part of our journey together, I'd like to honor a simple and profound shift that is taking place. This shift is one from passive learning to self-responsibility and personal empowerment.

In contrast to a course, program or workshop that gives everyone who attends a prescribed model, the Finding Your Flow process here is designed to help you devise your own developmental journey.

Perhaps you remember with great detail the years comprising your formal education. Sitting in tight rows, facing forward, taking notes, and learning precisely what your neighbor was learning. There was one teacher, one method, and everybody was expected to demonstrate that knowledge to the teacher who would grade you and tell you how well you did compared to the others in your class.

Was this process designed with your specific needs, wants, and aspirations in mind? Not usually. In fact, that learning process was designed to serve the middle of the bell curve—the masses—in the most efficient way possible. Perhaps you felt underserved by this shotgun approach, more like a passive receiver of knowledge rather than an active participant.

Let's fast-forward to a time when you discovered something of great interest to you. Do you remember this time—a time when you made that shift from passive learner to active participant in your learning? Did you seek out knowledge yourself, find books, talk to people, experiment with ideas, test your theories, or simply plunge into a topic because it turned you on, filled you up and inspired you? If so, you made the shift, you lit your own fire, you took ownership for your own learning and your own growth.

Since our early years, most of us have been rewarded for passively absorbing what was fed to us. Our parents, teachers, coaches—with good intentions—filled us with what they knew. But that kind of learning never had the same power as when we discovered for ourselves the ideas, knowledge, and skills that truly served our core values and purpose. This was a process that each of us had to own for ourselves.

Finding Your Flow is all about taking an active role in your own personal development. While each one of us may benefit from the advice of experienced others, such outside help must take second place to our own awareness, learning and goal-setting. This empowerment now comes from the inside and not the outside. Malcolm Knowles, the well-known philosopher of adult learning, called this learning process "andragogy," which stipulates that:

1. Adults need to be involved in the planning and evaluation of their instruction.
2. Experience (including mistakes) provides the basis for learning activities.
3. Adults are most interested in learning subjects that have immediate relevance to their job or personal life, creating readiness to learn.
4. Adult learning is problem-centered rather than content-oriented.[55]

As adults, we play the key role in our own learning. We finally become our own coach, shrink, and guru as we take on the role for designing a learning plan that is best for us. And while the "how" of finding your flow may very well be expert-driven, the "what" is a very personal process—one that is best left to you.

While you may always gather information and feedback, only you can conduct your 720° sweep and assess your Flow Assets and Liabilities on a continuing basis. You are now your own best coach. And who better to do the job?

Building a Life of Flow

We have spent this entire book defining, understanding, assessing, sorting, and identifying the many flow assets and liabilities that impact your ability to find and sustain the moments of flow in your life. In many respects, this book has been about singling out and illuminating those special moments. I hope you will now realize that all this has not been only about the special moments, but about every moment—past, present, and future.

Consider the number 788,400. Does it have any particular meaning to you? Given advances in modern medicine, and if luck is on your side, this is somewhere close to the number of hours you will live if you make it to the age of 90. Consider those 32,850 days, 788,400 hours, or 47,304,000 minutes. How many of these moments have you already spent? How many do you have left?

Finding Your Flow is quite simply about engineering the moments of your life and making the most out of them. It is the recognition that we prepare for each moment, we enter each moment, then exit each moment. Through this process we extract the lessons and learnings out of each one of them, and then, armed with new life experience, prepare for the next moment.

Flow is much like an hour glass where each grain of sand, representing a performance moment, gets closer and closer to the bottleneck (a moment that is just about to happen), then as it reaches the apex, the moment you are experiencing right now, the sand rushes through only to land on the increasingly large pile below (the moments you have already collected in your life).

Finding Your Flow is a way of looking at your life and asking yourself: "Am I making the most of every moment that I have on this earth? Am I making the most of my time, living to my full potential, and becoming the person I most want to become— every day and every hour?

As we break down the days of our lives, it is easy to see just how much time is spent on seemingly trivial pursuits. We awake in the mornings, which for each of us includes many daily rituals of washing and preparing. We eat, drive to work or school, we work or study, eat again, walk, talk, chat with friends and colleagues, perhaps exercise, drive home, eat again, watch TV, surf the Internet, conduct similar preparations for bed, and then we sleep. This might be a bit simplistic but not too off the mark. So when do we find our flow during these days? In fact, we can find more flow in every part of our day. The more Flow Assets we have in place, the higher probability that we will find our flow in all of the little and big moments of our lives.

If you have ever witnessed or read about the art and practice of the Japanese Tea Ceremony, you know that the entire process is one of intent, focus, mindfulness and flow. From entering the room, to the preparation of the tea, to the sipping of the tea, each phase of each moment is designed with pure intent so that not a second is lost to trivial thinking or acting. The goal of this ceremony is to be completely at one with the moment—even if every moment is simply about the preparation, drinking, and exiting of the tea ceremony experience. Regardless of the activity, flow is about being focused and absorbed in the moment. Consider the following Japanese proverb:

If man has no tea in him,
he is incapable of understanding truth and beauty.

In essence, having tea within you is your capacity to find, sustain, and cultivate every moment within every life arena. Certainly, you may look at much of your day and find it trivial and not very flowing. Instead you may consider only the bigger moments— giving a presentation, taking an exam, making a sale, participating in a competition, creating something—as ones worthy of applying the strategies for flow. But this is a significant mistake. Don't sell yourself short on the great opportunity to live every moment with intent, purpose, and enjoyment.

When you awake, do so with intent and joy in your heart. When you step into the shower, set a goal to visualize the day. When you dress, focus on each phase of the process and nothing else. When you walk to the kitchen do so by noticing each step. When you eat savor each bite. When you make your way to work notice the world around you, seek awareness, practice generating positive thoughts and emotions, picture the day from beginning to end, get lost in a song or the news. When you work, take one small task at a time and get completely lost in it—focusing on the most important thing each minute—each hour. When you connect with others, look at them with new eyes, see their uniqueness, listen deeply to them, seek to learn and understand who they really are and what they truly need. When you exercise, do so with a clear goal in mind, tap into your heartbeat, notice the heat of your body, take in the immediate surroundings, the temperature, the smells, the sounds.

When the end of the day nears, ponder what you learned and how you grew that day. Notice the things you did that helped you grow as a person and learn from mistakes. Look for new perspectives that help you find the positive in every challenge and frustration. Be grateful for this process, knowing that today you are better than you were yesterday.

Like many of the skills we tend to lose as we grow out of childhood, flow is something we can re-capture. This book was designed to help you recognize that flow is a natural part of life. Let this be a starting point for your ongoing awareness of what helps and hinders flow for you. By inviting more flow into your life, you may discover the true potential that lies deep within you.

Appendices

Appendix A: Method and Procedures for Identifying Flow Arenas and Strategies: Reflections on the Research

In my study of flow I was struck by the fact that the building blocks of flow seemed limited to under a dozen factors or descriptors. But how could this be? As we're the world's most complex species, and as I sought to understand one of the most complex of human experiences, I reasoned that there had to more to it than what had already been discovered and written about in the books and scientific articles. Thus began my research journey.

My research question can be broken down into three parts. First, where do individuals experience flow? Second, when they discover this experience, what strategies do they use to propel themselves into flow? And third, do flow strategies differ based on age and experience? My hypothesis was that flow could manifest itself in any activity and that strategies for initiating and sustaining flow could be understood and learned.

To explore these questions, I pre-interviewed dozens of individuals to discuss their flow experiences with them, then more specifically to talk with them about the practical strategies that they used to get into flow more often. Once it was clear that people loved to talk about their experiences and could fairly easily describe where they had them and what they did to re-create them—or try to re-create them—I began looking for subjects who were willing to talk in more depth about their experiences.

In my study I interviewed 64 individuals ranging from 15 to 95 years of age. I then completed a qualitative review of the more than 700 pages of raw interview data and boiled each question down into core themes, identifying the many arenas and strategies used by the interviewees to find their flow.

In discussing their experiences with them, my hypothesis was confirmed. It seemed that no matter what somebody was doing, it was possible for a flow experience to occur. With the 64 individuals studied, I counted as many as 128 different flow arenas. Some discussed their experiences while playing sports. A young pediatric physician spoke of finding flow through the use of organizational strategies. Another found flow while reading a book, setting up a comfortable environment with the perfect lighting and just the right kind of motivation. Another found flow when walking through the forest hunting for wild mushrooms. Some found their flow while getting lost in an art project. Others found their flow when playing in the sandbox with their children, gardening, sailing, teaching, driving, walking in the mountains. You name it and someone found flow while doing it.

Even more exciting for me was the discussion surrounding my subjects' personal strategies. Through these and other interviews and discussions, more than 150 different flow strategies were discussed. These strategies can be organized into approximately eleven major themes with multiple sub-themes. Below is the model that represents the clustering of these flow strategy themes:

Choosing the Right Environment

Placing oneself in an environment that is conductive to generating a flow experience (i.e., a dance hall, operating room, office, the mountains etc...).

Environment Regulation

Regulating the environment to enhance or support a flow experience (i.e., changing temperature, lighting, furniture arrangement, etc...).

Interpersonal Regulation

Managing life relationships to decrease inter-personal interferences, allowing one to have greater levels of focus.

— Spiritual Strategies

Strategies of the spirit - primarily to engage higher forces (i.e., prayer, humility, deeper purposes of self, etc...)

— Philosophical Strategies

Strategies of philosophy (i.e., beliefs, principles, attitudes, perspectives, rules, standards, etc...).

— Psychological Strategies

Strategies of the mind (i.e., goals, self-talk, focus, visualization, etc...)

— Emotional Strategies

Strategies of the heart - primarily generating the right affect or mood.

— Physical Strategies

Strategies of the body - primarily for raising or lowering arousal.

Self Regulation Strategies

Effort Regulation

Choosing when and how to enter flow, managing personal state during flow

Preparation

General preparation, practice and administration, prior to the flow experience.

Personal Management

General life management strategies (i.e., ample sleep, nutrition, massages, and other general health concerns etc..., in order to build a base-line of wellness.

161

Appendix B: Top 20 Flow Strategies and the Principles of Personal Excellence Course

People often ask me what are the most prevalent strategies my research turned up for entering flow. What follows are the top 20 areas of study that are often at the heart of flow and any serious peak performance training program. These strategic development arenas have been organized and built into a course called The Principles of Personal Excellence. The core content of the course includes the following principles, concepts and ideas that help support flow as a constant companion:

1. Locus of Control:
    Flow seekers know what it means to control the controllable. They have learned to let go of everything outside of their influence and focus in specifically on the things that make the big difference.

2. Physical Foundations:
    Flow seekers eat well, take care of their bodies through physical training, get adequate sleep, and take time to recover.

3. Motives, Values & Purpose
    Flow seekers tap into resources of energy. They recognize what motivates them and they know how to make use of that motivation. Flow seekers know and understand their core values, they tap into both internal and external sources of motivation— motivation that usually takes them beyond their own self-interest and focuses on something bigger than themselves. This allows them to lose their ego and be completely absorbed in the activity at hand.

4. Mission, Vision & Legacy

Flow seekers know what they want. Their mission is clear. With these boundaries in place they have a clear picture of the desired outcome. They can see this picture from every angle: from the future, from the present, and from the past. It is an image—even a multi-dimensional image—that stays with them until it has been fulfilled.

5. Philosophy/Ethos

Flow seekers live by a clearly defined philosophy. They have clarified and understand the beliefs, principles, attitudes, perspectives, qualities, virtues, rules and standards that govern each and every moment of their lives. This philosophy keeps them grounded, giving them a base of consistency which allows them to return and repeat their performances with equal or greater zeal.

6. Goals (building an architecture of focus)

Flow seekers know how to take their objectives from the 50,000-foot level to the ground floor. They do this by the proper setting of goals by time and distance. They know how to set life-long goals as well as intermediate and short-term goals that focus attention on the present moment.

7. Measurement/Scorecarding

Flow seekers know how to measure their success and keep score within the game of life that they are playing. Doing this on a consistent basis provides the feedback necessary to change course and re-adjust strategy.

8. Perception Management

Flow seekers master the art of thinking and processing information. They know that the quality of their interpretation of the world around them will equal the quality of their life. They know how to see the world through clean lenses, they avoid neurotic and distorted thinking. Instead they focus on what is true and real, and they meet their challenges with a positive yet realistic frame of mind.

9. Visualization

Flow seekers know how to visualize what they want. They imagine mental pictures of the outcomes they want and they burn these pictures in their mind everyday. With such imagery filling their every waking moment, they move ever closer to that reality.

10. Internal Dialogue

Flow seekers are compelled to not only manage but to produce the thoughts and attitudes that support high levels of focus. Instead of allowing their internal dialogue to detract from their current focus, they use it to cultivate the attitudes that support present moment focus. From positive self-talk to affirmations or compelling personal questions, the flow seeker is a master at monitoring and controlling thought.

11. Managing Time

Flow seekers recognize that getting into flow means a proper stage-setting to insure that their attention is completely absorbed in the task at hand. To insure this they are masters at preparing for the moment.

12. Managing Space

Flow seekers know what it means to organize resources, place everything in its proper order and minimize distractions to stay completely in the moment.

13. Emotional Intelligence

Flow seekers understand the value of emotional control, which is invariably connected with thought processing and internal dialogue. High performers use their emotions to their advantage. Emotions such as fear, self-doubt, anxiety, and anger are kept in check and are instead used as feedback and for rational decision-making. Equally important is the ability to generate positive emotions—even feelings of high self-confidence on demand—to keep focusing attention squarely on the present moment.

14. Physical Control

From mastering the art of breathing to controlling physical states through progressive relaxation, as well as autogenic training and other strategies, flow seekers are experts at controlling their bodies and maintaining a sense of calm and control that sustains focus and increases energy. Taken together these strategies help them find the precise arousal state that taps into the moment.

15. Rituals and Routines

Getting into the moment is often ushered in by the proper sequencing of actions. These pre-performance habits, personal to each individual, help flow seekers fall into flow by tapping into established patterns of behavior.

16. Planning & Preparation

Clarifying your performance goals, organizing your resources, visualizing the outcome you wish to have, building contingency plans, and so on, are all part of preparation and planning. Flow finders know each of the questions to ask and have their own ways of making sure that peak performance and flow are ready to happen.

17. Focus

Flow finders understand where their attention is, and spend the right amount where it is needed, allowing them the luxury of centering themselves, putting all of their resources in the present moment and executing that moment with full and complete engagement.

18. Processing Experiences & Engaging Feedback
Flow finders never let such experiences go to waste, processing and learning from every one of them. These learnings are used as feedback to enhance the process and add strategies for future use.

19. Self-Image and Self-Confidence Building
Flow finders recognize that moments of flow support effective habit formation. These experiences form the basis of their self-image, self-confidence, the formation of personal values, and ultimately their character. Each experience further expands their perspective and furthers the development of their personal philosophy.

20. The Recognition of Becomingness
Flow finders recognize that flow is not just about the moment itself, but the collection of moments throughout their lives. They also recognize that it's not only about achieving peak states of performance, but rather about using flow as a benchmark or quality standard. They consider all 788,400 of life's precious hours. Will you spend your hours, days, months and years having these moments for the benefit of yourself—where you take more out of this world than you put in? If so, consider yourself in the negative (--) category. Perhaps you have added to the world to the degree you have taken away or consumed it. If so, consider yourself in the neutral (0) category. Perhaps you have discovered that Finding Your Flow is not just for the benefit of self, but for the betterment of the world around you. Perhaps you have discovered that true happiness comes from serving in Meaningful Life Arenas that help you fulfill your true gifts and talents,

yet serve a calling that is bigger than yourself. If you have discovered this secret to life, then consider yourself in the positive (+) column—a flow finder with a destiny.

Putting these top 20+ strategies together yields an hourglass representing the passing of time and the collection of experiences. Whatever your "one thing" is currently, learning to understand and master these top 20 strategic arenas will take you a long way towards finding your flow in all your Meaningful Life Arenas.

THE PREPARATION AND PROCESSING OF EXPERIENCE

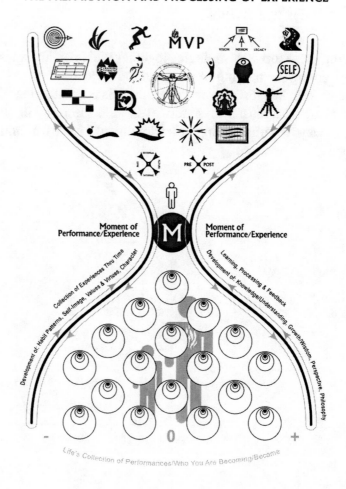

As you collect these moments, you come to recognize that flow is a way of life. It is the quality factor that helps you maximize your experience no matter what you are doing. You can now ready yourself for the moment, be completely absorbed in that moment, and then exit that moment with greater joy and insight than you had before. With this mindset in place, you cannot only find your flow, but you can have it for the rest of your life.

If you are interested in taking the complete "Principles of Personal Excellence" course, please visit my web-site at: www.theiahe.com for more information.

Appendix C: Blank Score Cards

Life Arena:

SMART Goal 1:

Date Engaged:	Expected Completion Date:	Date Completed:

Expected benefits of goal:

Expected benefits of goal:

Expected benefits of goal:

Strategic Action Steps:	Start Date:	End Date:
1		
2		
3		
4		
5		
6		

Source of Process Feedback: Frequency of Feedback:

Source of Outcome Feedback: Frequency of Feedback:

OM

Process Measure:

Day	1	2	3	4	5	6	7	8	9	10	11	12	13	14	15	16	17	18	19	20	21	22	23	24	25	26	27	28	29	30	31

Daily Progress

Milestone 1:	Celebration 1:
Milestone 2:	Celebration 2:
Milestone 3:	Celebration 3:
Milestone 4:	Celebration 4:
Milestone 5:	Celebration 5:

Goal Achieved:	Grand Celebration:

Adapted from The Game of Work. Park City, Utah

170

Life Arena:

SMART Goal 1:

Date Engaged:	Expected Completion Date:	Date Completed:

Expected benefits of goal:
Expected benefits of goal:
Expected benefits of goal:

Strategic Action Steps:	Start Date:	End Date:
1		
2		
3		
4		
5		
6		

Source of Process Feedback:	Frequency of Feedback:
Source of Outcome Feedback:	Frequency of Feedback:

OM

Process Measure:

Day	1	2	3	4	5	6	7	8	9	10	11	12	13	14	15	16	17	18	19	20	21	22	23	24	25	26	27	28	29	30	31

Daily Progress

Milestone 1:	Celebration 1:
Milestone 2:	Celebration 2:
Milestone 3:	Celebration 3:
Milestone 4:	Celebration 4:
Milestone 5:	Celebration 5:

Goal Achieved:	Grand Celebration:

Life Arena:

SMART Goal 1:

Date Engaged:	Expected Completion Date:	Date Completed:
Expected benefits of goal:		
Expected benefits of goal:		
Expected benefits of goal:		

Strategic Action Steps:	Start Date:	End Date:
1		
2		
3		
4		
5		
6		

Source of Process Feedback:	Frequency of Feedback:
Source of Outcome Feedback:	Frequency of Feedback:

OM

Process Measure:

Day	1	2	3	4	5	6	7	8	9	10	11	12	13	14	15	16	17	18	19	20	21	22	23	24	25	26	27	28	29	30	31

Daily Progress

Milestone 1:	Celebration 1:
Milestone 2:	Celebration 2:
Milestone 3:	Celebration 3:
Milestone 4:	Celebration 4:
Milestone 5:	Celebration 5:

Goal Achieved:	Grand Celebration:

Adapted from The Game of Work, Park City, Utah

172

BIBLIOGRAPHY

Barden, R. C., Jackson, B. H. & Ford, M. (1992). **Optimal performance in tennis**. Minneapolis: OPS Press.

Burton, D. (1993). Goal setting in sport. In R.N. Singer, M. Murphey & L. K. Tennant, **Handbook of research on sport psychology**. New York: Macmillan (pp. 467-491).

Capra, F. (1996). **The web of life**. New York: Anchor Books.

Chidester, T. R. & Grigsby, W. C. (1984). **A meta-analysis of the goal setting performance literature**. Academy of Management Proceedings, Ada, Ohio.

Coonradt, C. (1984). **The game of work**. Salt Lake City: Shadow Mountains.

Crews, D. J. (1993). Self-regulation strategies in sport and exercise. (In R. N. Singer, M. Murphey & L.K. Tennant, Eds.). **Handbook of research on sport psychology** (pp. 557-570). New York: Macmillan.

Csikszentmihalyi, M. (1975). **Beyond boredom and anxiety**. San Francisco: Jossey-Bass Publishers.

Csikszentmihalyi, M. (1985). Reflection on enjoyment. **Perspectives in Biology and Medicine**, 28(4), 489-497.

Csikszentmihalyi, M. (1990). **Flow**. New York: Harper Collins.

Csikszentmihalyi, M. (1997). **Finding flow: The psychology of engagement with everyday life**. New York: Basic Books.

Csikszentmihalyi, M. & Csikszentmihalyi, I. (1988). **Optimal experience**: Cambridge: Cambridge University Press.

Csikszentmihalyi, M. & LeFevre, J. (1989). Optimal experience in work and leisure. **Journal of Personality and Social Psychology, 56**(5), 815-22.

Duval, S. & Wicklund (1972). **A theory of objective self-awareness**. New York: Academic Press.

Fine, A. (1993). **Mind over golf**. London: BBC Books.

Fredrick, M. J. (1999). **Peak moments in sport karate tournament competition: Black belt fighters in the zone**. Unpublished doctoral dissertation. The University of Utah, Salt Lake City, UT.

Gallwey, W. T. (1974). **The inner game of tennis**. London: Pan Books.

Geist, S. (2003). Would you work for you? **Performance Improvement, 42**(3), 5-13.

Gladwell, M. (2008). **Outliers: the story of success**. New York: Little, Brown and Company.

Gleick, J. (1987). **Chaos**. New York: Penguin Books.

Hallowell, E. M. & Ratey, J. (1994). **Driven to distraction: Recognizing and coping with attention deficit disorder from childhood through adulthood**. New York: Touchstone.

Hamilton, J. A. (1981). Attention, personality, and the self-regulation of mood: Absorbing interest and boredom. **Progress in Experimental Personality Research, 10**, 281-315.

Herrigel, E. (1953). **Zen and the art of archery**. New York: Vintage Books.

Holcomb, J. H. (1976). Attention and intrinsic rewards in the control of psychophysiologic states. **Psychotherapy and Psychosomatics, 27,** 54-61.

Holland, J. H. (1995). **Hidden order**. Reading, Massachusetts: Addison-Wesley Publishing.

Jackson, S. A. (1992). **Elite athletes in flow: The psychology of optimal experience**. Unpublished doctoral dissertation, University of North Carolina, Greensboro, North Carolina.

Jackson, S. A., & Csikszentmihalyi, M. (1999). **Flow in sports**. Champaign, IL: Human Kinetics.

Kaplan, R. S. & Norton, D. P. (1996). **The balanced scorecard**. Boston: Harvard Business School Press.

Locke, E. A. & Latham, G. P. (1990). **A theory of goal setting and task performance**. Englewood Cliffs, NJ: Prentice-Hall.

Loehr, J. E. (1986). **Mental toughness training for sports**. New York: Penguin Group.

Maslow, A. (1954). **Motivation and personality**. New York: Harper & Row.

Massimini, F. & Carli, M. (1988). The systematic assessment of flow in daily experience. In M. Csikszentmihalyi & I. S. Csikszentmihalyi, **Optimal Experience: Psychological studies of flow in consciousness** (pp. 266-278). Cambridge: Cambridge University Press.

Mikulas, W. L. & Vodanovich, S. J. (1993). The essence of boredom. **The Psychological Record, 43,** 3-12.

175

McWhinney, W. (1993). **Of paradigms and system theories**. The Fielding Graduate Institute, Santa Barbara, CA.

Mundell, C. E. (2000). **The role of perceived skill, perceived challenge, and flow in the experience of positive and negative affect**. Unpublished doctoral dissertation. George Mason University, Washington, D.C.

Murphy, M. & Brodie, J. (1973). I experience a kind of clarity. **Intellectual Digest, 5**, 19-22.

Orlick, T. (1990). **In pursuit of excellence**. Champaign, Illinois: Leisure Press.

Orlick, T. (1991). Optimizing individual performance. In D. Druckman & R. Bjork, **The mind's eye: Enhancing human performance** (pp. 193-246). Washington, D.C.: National Academy Press.

Perry, S. K. (1999). **Writing in flow: Keys to enhanced creativity**. Cincinnati, OH: Writer's Digest Books.

Ross, N. W. (1960). **The world of Zen**. New York: Vintage Books.

Sansone, C., Wier, C., Harpster, L. & Morgan, C. (1992). Once a boring task always a boring task? Interest as a self-regulatory mechanism. **Journal of Personality and Social Psychology, 63**(3), 379-390.

Selye, H. (1976). **The stress of life.** New York, NY: McGraw-Hill.

Williams, J. M. (Ed). (1993). **Applied sport psychology: Personal growth to peak performance**. Mayfield, California: Mayfield Publishing Company.

ENDNOTES

[1] (Fredrick, 1999)

[2] (Williams, 1993)

[3] (Mundell, 2000)

[4] (Csikszentmihalyi & Csikszentmihalyi, 1988)

[5] (Csikszentmihalyi, 1975)

[6] (Csikszentmihalyi & Csikszentmihalyi, 1988)

[7] (Massimini & Carli, 1988)

[8] Csikszentmihalyi, 1985. pp. 490-491)

[9] (Hamilton, 1981, p. 289)

[10] (Csikszentmihalyi, 1997, p. 32)

[11] (Gladwell, 2008)

[12] The actual number of flow components is somewhat disputed. However, several sources discuss nine components.

[13] (Jackson, 1992)

[14] (Capra, 1996; Gleick, 1987; Holland, 1995; McWhinney, 1993)

[15] (Coonradt, 1984; Kaplan & Norton, 1996)

[16] (Duval and Wicklund, 1972)

[17] (Mundell, 2000)

[18] (Perry, 1999, p. 20)

[19] (Orlick, 1990, p. 157)

[20] (Fine, 1993)

[21] (Gallwey, 1974)

[22] (Murphy and Brodie, 1973, p. 19)

[23] (Csikszentmihalyi, 1975, p. 10)

[24] (Csikszentmihalyi, 1997, p.26)

[25] (Hallowell & Ratey, 1994)

[26] (Jackson & Csikszentmihalyi, 1999, p. 20)

[27] (Suzuki, 1998, 94, 96)

[28] (Csikszentmihalyi, 1975, 1990, 1996; Csikszentmihalyi & Csikszentmihalyi, 1988, Csikszentmihalyi et al., 1993; Jackson & Csikszentmihalyi, 1999; Perry, 1999).

[29] (The juggling experience demonstration is courtesy of InsideOut Development, LLC)

[30] (Orlick, 1990, p. 157)

[31] Ibid

[32] (Csikszentmihalyi & LeFevre, 1989)

[33] (Herrigel, 1953)

[34] (Ross, 1960)

[35] (Holcomb, 1977; Mikulas and Vodanovich, 1993)

[36] (Sansone et al., 1992)

[37] (Givens, 1993)

[38] (Locke and Latham, 1990)

[39] (Burton, 1993, Pg. 469)

[40] (Chidester & Grigsby, 1984)

[41] (Stein & Book, 2000)

[42] (Selye, 1956)

[43] (Barden, Jackson & Ford, 1992)

[44] (Loehr, 1986)

[45] (Orlick, 1990)

[46] (Csikszentmihalyi & Csikszentmihalyi, 1988, p. 31)

[47] (Crews & Boutcher, 1986, p. 291)

[48] (Perry, 1999)

[49] (Geist, 2003)

[50] (Maslow, 1954)

[51] (Orlick, 1991)

[52] (Dr. Robert Nidiffer discussed this 4-quadrant model in his work with athletes)

[53] (http://www.ehmac.ca/everything-else-eh/69058-superstitious-athletes-strange-sports-rituals.html)

[54] (Fritz, Brown, Lunde & Banset, 2005)

[55] (http://encyclopedia.thefreedictionary.com/Andragogy)

ABOUT THE AUTHOR

As a practitioner and student of applied human performance technologies, Dr. Jackson is dedicated to the ongoing development of individuals, teams, and organizations. He has worked with young athletes, inner-city children, and Fortune 500 companies alike—recognizing that the principles of personal excellence and performance are as valid for the aspiring student as for the CEO.

Dr. Jackson is a certified member of the United States Professional Tennis Association and the Professional Ski Instructors of America. He holds Master's degrees in Counseling Psychology from Boston University School of Education; in Business Administration from University of Minnesota Carlson School of Management; and in Organizational Development from Fielding Graduate University. He earned his Ph.D. in Human and Organizational Systems from Fielding Graduate University where his research identifies many of the core components and strategies people use to search for and replicate peak experiences.

Dr. Jackson served as the Director of The Center for the Advancement of Leadership at Utah Valley University—a leading organization in the study and practice of youth and adult leadership development. He also directs the C. Charles Jackson Foundation whose focus is to promote leadership, character, and life-skills development for youth throughout the U.S. He also serves as the CEO of The Institute of Applied Human Excellence, a training firm dedicated to helping individuals, teams, and organizations find their peak performances through flow.

As writer, speaker, author, consultant, coach, and leadership adventure facilitator, Dr. Jackson helps individuals seek their highest capacities while fulfilling meaningful life missions. You can reach Dr. Jackson at:

Dr. Bruce H. Jackson
The Institute of Applied Human Excellence
www.theiahe.com
brucehjackson@gmail.com
801-358-8450

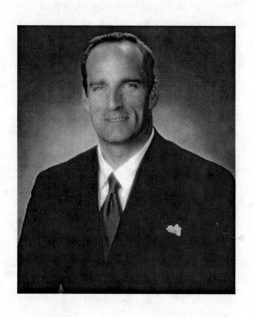